Investing in real estate:

A guide for beginners to generate long-term passive income from property

5 steps towards your financial independence: rent, buy, rehab, refinance and repeat

(RBRRR strategy)

CONTENTS

INTRODUCTION vi
CHAPTER I 1
   Introduction to Real Estate 1
      Benefits of Rental Property Investment 4
      Real Estate Investing: Buying and Selling at the Right Time 6
      The Biggest Mistake: Having an Unclear Property Investment Strategy 7
CHAPTER II 16
   How RBRRR works 16
      Tips for Diversifying Your Portfolio 23
      What Is Diversification? 23
      Uses of RBRRR Strategy 26
      Top of the List Risk Mitigations 30
CHAPTER III 36
   HOW TO DETERMINE A GOOD RENTAL PROPERTY 36
      Step by step instructions to know a Good Rental Property 43
      The most effective method to Determine If a Multifamily Property Is a Good Investment 48
CHAPTER IV 53
   HOW TO DETERMINE WHAT TYPE OF RENTAL TO BUY 53
      Instructions to Buy Investment Rental Property 55
      Properties of Rental Investment: Time to Buy or Sell 57

    Step by step instructions to Buy an Investment Property 57

    At the point when to sell a Rental Property 58

CHAPTER V 66
    HOW TO FIND LOW COST PROPERTIES 66

    Steps to Finding Low Risk Investments When Buying Rental Property 68

    The most effective method to Spot Good Locations .. 73

    What Type of Rental Property Should I Buy? 75

    Instructions to Analyze Investment Properties 76

CHAPTER VI 80
    HOW TO FINANCE RENTALS 80

    Innovative Methods for Financing a Rental Property Purchase 82

    Financing Five to Ten Rental Properties 87

CHAPTER VII 91
    HOW TO REPAIR AND MAINTAIN PROPERTIES 91

    The Role and Responsibilities of a Rental Property Manager 92

    Protection and Ongoing Maintenance 93

CHAPTER VIII 101
    HOW TO RECRUIT TOP TALENT TO WORK ON YOUR PROPERTY 101

CHAPTER IX 112
    HOW TO MANAGE RENTALS OR FIND A PROPERTY MANAGER 112

CHAPTER X 135

THE BEST EXIT STRATEGIES TO CONSIDER 135

What Is a Real Estate Exit system? 135

The Importance of a Real Estate Exit Strategy 136

Top Real Estate Exit Strategies 137

INTRODUCTION

Rental property investment is rising as an amazing choice for investors as they are on edge about the unexpected droops and piddling additions of the securities exchange.

If it is true that you are searching for rental property investment, then so much caution must be taken. Before you set on your journey for a rental property, guarantee that you really comprehend what it resembles to be a landowner. In spite of the fact that it is a gainful endeavor, it's anything but a snap using any and all means. You would need to keep up the property so as to receive the monetary benefits all through the time of your ownership.

To many, rental property investment is basically something that includes purchasing a house, giving it on lease, and after that rounding up bucks while unwinding in a sofa. Notwithstanding, this is a long way from being realistic, particularly, in the event that you wish for a normal rental pay for a considerable length of time to come. Stowing a rental property and accumulating a sound rental salary for a year or two is only a commonplace undertaking. In any case, keeping up an enduring rental salary until you sell the property is the thing that considers an extraordinary exertion on your part.

Being an investor, there is nothing more awful than keeping an empty rental property. This is on the grounds that you would at present need assets for the upkeep of the property, which isn't giving you any profits as its empty. Consequently, you ought to effectively look for inhabitants, and do whatever is conceivable to keep them placated. This includes paying attention to the requirements of the inhabitants and making convenient fixes. In spite of the fact that you may do some paltry fixes without anyone else's input, other complex undertakings (fixing channel holes and windowpanes) are best left to a specialist.

As you continue to look for rental property investment, it is essential that you think about the area. This involves considering the separation of the property from your living arrangement, the accessibility of inhabitants, the normal lease that you can gather, and the capacity of occupants in the region to pay you. A few districts may demonstrate more helpful than others. For example, it is smarter to lease a house close by a school, since a dreadful parcel of understudies are probably going to scan for an abode in the region of their school. This outcomes in a plentiful inventory of occupants throughout the entire year. In a substance, rental property investment is tied in with investigating the area, taking the necessary steps to lease your property, keeping your inhabitants cheerful, and keeping up the property so it tends to be leased quite a long time after year in this way limiting the opportunity time frame.

Investment in rental property can be a dangerous recommendation if the investor has not done his/her study well. In any case, for the investor who has set aside the effort to look into, it tends to be rewarding. Presumably the one thing most investors need to know more than everything else is the means by which they can wind up affluent in the briefest timeframe putting resources into rental property.

Most investors are caught up with focusing on flipping single-family houses, when they ought to focus on putting resources into multi-nuclear families. With a solitary family house on the off chance that you lose the leaseholder you have lost 100% of your salary, which could be your benefit for a whole year. On the off chance that you have a four-family condo and lose a tenant, you have three different families giving you checks to pay your costs. The primary concern is income and income is more prominent with multi-nuclear families than with single-nuclear families.

In the event that you have put resources into a few single-family rental properties you will more than likely need to make a trip to a few distinct areas to gather installments, or to mind the property. With one multi-nuclear family you spare time, gas and mileage on your auto by just going to one area to gather a few installments, or to keep an eye on your property. With the present economy it could cost from $2000-$7500 relying upon where in the nation it is arranged and the size of the house. Increase that by six and you're talking an extremely huge measure of cash. Fixing a six-family rooftop would cost between $5000-$10,000. You can figure it out.

There are a great deal of real estate master's with infomercials resigning the cash to be produced using flipping houses. They cause it to appear to be simple. You will before long observe it tends to be exorbitant rehabbing a house, particularly on the off chance that you don't check the house outstandingly a long time before purchasing. Costly, yet very tedious. Also, the various temporary workers you need to manage. That is another issue; setting aside the effort to meeting and research every one of those temporary workers. All things considered, you need somebody who knows what they are doing, isn't that right? When you locate a decent temporary worker and he has done work for you, don't figure they will consistently be prepared to hop when you call them. All things considered, they are specialists and they can't lounge around looking out for your calls. They have different irons in the flame like all great representatives.

Try not to misunderstand me, investment in rental property is a decent business. Single-family houses are wise investments. Yet, they can likewise be a way to putting resources into condos. On the off chance that you are aware of any individual who is making cash flipping houses, chances are great that the person additionally has a few condos in their portfolio. Flipping houses is fine for the individual who needs to do it, however investment in rental property is the better investment. Furthermore, there is an enormous market for condo contributing. Investment in rental property is a sound business.

The central objectives of any property investment are gratefulness, income and expense reserve funds. Rental property investment is the main property investment that gives all of you these three advantages simultaneously.

The primary rental property classes comprise of single family rental properties, multi-unit private rental properties, business rental properties and occasion homes. The primary class incorporates long haul single family leasing, the subsequent classification incorporates lofts, and structures for various families while the last class incorporates strip malls, places of business and so forth for a long haul leasing reason. Here are different focuses to consider with real property investments:

1) Methods like repossessions, monstrous homes, and probate homes are helpful for purchasing property. Rent buys can be very valuable which help you to use investment cash and arrive at a positive income from leasing. Purchasing fixer upper homes or repossessions can lessen investment cash and improve income and appreciation.

2) One can't expect an impressive income from property with one inhabitant. For this situation, the fundamental objective is to cover the home loan and current costs.

3) Research on a potential rental home ought to incorporate critical money related making arrangements for years

ahead, similar to costs of property management, fixing, opportunity, crisis and so on.

4) The condo and the 2-4 unit homes are the fundamental classes of the multi-unit private property investments.

5) With condo investments the fundamental benefit originates from the rental income. A rent to buy alternative and utilizing investment cash is very helpful for this situation. The most noteworthy factors for this situation are the money related assessment and property management. With an unfaltering income from various inhabitants, it is conceivable to procure a director for the property management. It expands the income and the estimation of the condo building. Underestimation may harm the investment and lead to misfortune.

6) Commercial properties investments incorporate places of business, retail malls, mechanical properties and so forth. The market estimation of these properties is settled on the income (net rental pay). The fundamental goal of rental in these cases is to create enough money to surpass the expense of home loan, protection, upkeep, future enhancements. This isn't a simple assignment to deal with. It requires investigation of numerous things. Yet, whenever done appropriately it could demonstrate to be worthwhile. Changes in the financial conditions typically pronouncedly affect these sorts of real estate investments than on private property investments. Furthermore, as places of business and mechanical properties are progressively vulnerable to these changes, it is shrewd to keep additional money to help those investments if something does not go true to form. For this situation, a cash utilizing approach (rent to buy alternative) is helpful.

7) An occasion home can be utilized in two different ways. It tends to be a property home or an investment property.

This classification incorporates resort properties, mountain homes, or shoreline homes. With occasion rentals, the fundamental benefit originates from the appreciation. Income produced from leasing is typically utilized for current costs like property management, home loan and protection. These are transient rentals and require escalated upkeep.

CHAPTER I
INTRODUCTION TO REAL ESTATE

There are numerous approaches to profit in real estate, yet putting resources into rental properties is by a long shot the most worthwhile, offering investors a twofold investment return; an unfaltering leftover pay from the month to month rental and the value from the property itself. Building riches from rental property investments ought not to be messed with however; there are numerous interesting points before you buy your first property.

Search for properties that will require practically zero fixes to prepare it to lease, down time implies you will have no salary from the property until it is leased. It is likewise imperative to utilize an accounting report for every property that you mean to lease, this will demonstrate to you the amount you have put resources into the buy and fixes with the measure of return you can expect once the property is leased. Everything about your investment methodology ought to be all around arranged with consideration regarding the everyday management and upkeep just as rental contracts. It is a smart thought to likewise have a rundown of qualified repairmen to deal with any potential crisis circumstance. You ought to likewise inquire about the territory you intend to lease in. Knowing the individual and monetary atmosphere of the region will give you profitable data to enable you to decide whether the area is directly for you.

Properties in well-known occasional areas have the potential for higher rental rates and could likewise be leased week after week. Another incredible rental investment thought is business property, rental rates are quite often higher for this sort of property and most rentals of this sort require a long haul duty. Consider every conceivable rental property you see with its general potential for snappy benefit, and ask yourself; is this a perfect area for such a property? How rapidly can this property be prepared to lease? What is the aggregate sum I should contribute, and what is profit sum for my investment?

When you plan on acquiring your first rental property with a credit, at that point you should build up a spread sheet for the property you goal to buy. A commonplace spreadsheet will cover a year course of events and incorporate all pay and costs for the property; the greater part of this data can be found in your own monetary record you made for the property. Alongside your spreadsheet you should have a field-tested strategy that layouts your proposition to buy and keep up your rental property. Your strategy ought to incorporate the sort of property you intend to lease, how you mean to oversee and keep up your property and make sure to incorporate any data that demonstrates your capacity to be productive; a prevalent regular area or high traffic business or business property or other rental property with a high benefit potential. You will likewise need to incorporate how you expect to defeat any potential hindrances. Putting resources into rental properties for learners is a worthwhile way to accomplishing a long haul remaining pay.

To have a productive investment from your rental properties, powerful rental management is vital. The most significant activity for property owners and land masters is keep up the property in brilliant condition. Rental and property management may appear to be straightforward however it really requests fastidious thought and diligent work. Land masters may enlist an expert management firm to do all the diligent work or they can do it without anyone else's help.

Owners ought to recall that before leasing the property, they ought to guarantee that the spot is clean and good. Doing this draws new intrigue and request in potential inhabitants and fills in as a code of prohibitive consideration for occupants to be mindful of when living in the owner's property. In addition, they should ensure that there are no harms, glitches or breakdowns on machines, power and water sources. It's prudent to take depictions of each room from each point so they will fill in as references in the episode of any harms.

At the point when occupants are dwelling a property, it's significant for property owners to be mindful and auspicious in making a move to the inhabitant's solicitations and concerns, should the solicitations are reasonable enough. They are additionally obliged to do property assessments for any fixes fundamental and should the property require improvement.

When the occupants have moved away, owners should ensure that there's no harm to the property and that it has been left perfect and in a similar condition from the beginning. This makes it easier for them to get the property set and sorted out before the following occupant moves in. In the circumstance for harms, in the event that they go over the harm store sum, property owners reserve the privilege to request the extra add up to the inhabitants. Ensuring rental properties is profoundly basic for investment benefits.

In the event that property owners hand over their rental properties to proficient management specialists, they won't need to be disturbed by rental support and management employments in light of the fact that an expert property administrator will take all the fundamental managements for them. Their obligations and duties just focus on overseeing and looking after properties, keep the property brimming with occupants paying the most extreme measure of lease and to discover not too bad inhabitants that would think about the property with worth and regard.

It's essential to obtain most extreme benefits from any rental property. So land rulers and property owners ought to have the correct information and aptitude in overseeing and keeping up their rental properties in great condition.

Benefits of Rental Property Investment

With such a large number of points of interest to owning rental property, just as property management, an ever-increasing number of individuals are exploiting this investment. One of the significant focal points to owning rental property is that when you make this kind of investment buy, you have a substantial resource, as contrasted and different sorts of investments, for example, stocks and bonds. It is more clear the genuine worth and worth of your advantage when you can really observe it. Moreover, the standard rental salary that you get is effectively quantifiable, and you can ordinarily anticipate that it should proceed for quite a while.

A few people are worried about putting their cash into budgetary frameworks; be that as it may, so as to develop your riches and resource base, you're by and large needed to burn through cash. Real estate contributing is an incredible arrangement. The securities exchange is known to be very flighty, with continuous vacillations. Actually, real estate will in general remain genuinely solid, notwithstanding when the investment market debilitates to some degree. One reason that real estate keeps on being a wise investment even in a more fragile economy is that the more fragile economy frequently keeps numerous individuals from having the option to acquire a home loan making a bigger gathering of leaseholders to browse, since despite everything they need a protected and agreeable spot to live.

Rental property can deliver a normal pay, which is a colossal favorable position for some individuals. In spite of the fact that you do need to deduct the home loan installment from your all out salary (in the event that you have a home loan financed) just as support and fix costs, the property can regularly create a constant flow of pay for you.

Real estate can acknowledge in worth, contingent upon the market. After some time, numerous properties will wind up worth more, however this isn't really a certification yet is reliant on numerous variables, including area, kind of property and period of property, upkeep and different components. Putting resources into a steady territory will build the chances that your property will acknowledge in worth.

Influence alludes to the capacity to buy rental property utilizing cash that is obtained. When you can get the cash, you can stand to contribute more since you just need to put down a level of the all-out expense. Since the property itself will verify the obligation, and the rental salary will cover the home loan and duty costs, you remain to make bigger benefits.

Another bit of leeway to rental property is that you can take many expense reasoning identified with it. You can deduct the expense of upkeep and fixes, enhancements, charges, protection, contract intrigue, and the sky is the limit from there.

When you claim rental property, it is where you can work for yourself. This is a preferred position that many find alluring. Regardless of whether you are proposing to be low maintenance landowner or build up a profession in property management, you will profit by the capacity to settle on the major choices and experience the autonomy of owning your very own business.

Real Estate Investing: Buying and Selling at the Right Time

Real estate contributing could be summed up as "area, area, area," however similarly as significant is the planning and timing. Timing is particularly significant in real estate contributing in light of the fact that:

1) Exchanges can take quite a while, which requires arranging and premonition.
2) All real estate, in all business sectors, are remarkable, with dynamic and rapidly evolving powers.

Since purchasing or selling real estate is a complex and tedious procedure, you have to begin it off at the earliest opportunity. While you're trusting that the majority of the pieces will fall set up, the market can change, leaving you with botched chances for higher benefits. You should most likely prepare and see future valleys and tops in the real estate valuing to realize when to begin purchasing and when to begin selling.

Fixer upper properties can generally win you a decent benefit. That is on the grounds that essential fixes and support can expand a property's estimation by over 10%. On the off chance that you can do the fixes yourself, that is essentially benefit. You can likewise inquire about abandonment closeouts and houses that are headed to defaulting. In the event that you can strike on a decent property rapidly, you'll get it for less. What's more, in the event that you get the planning perfectly with your examination, you can discover an area on its approach to revitalization and see tremendous future cost increments. Neighborhood governments can likewise offer motivating forces for such territories as they have an enthusiasm for seeing it improve also.

In any case, to have the option to consummate that planning and exploit the above real estate contributing thoughts, you need capital close by. This implies you generally need financing close by. That doesn't need to be enormous wholes of cash in your investment account, which means strong credit, endorsed financing from banks and knowing the choices and breaking points for advances that you could get. At the point when different markets endure, savvy real estate contributing can generally make a benefit. You simply need to do the majority of your exploration and ideal the specialty of timing.

The Biggest Mistake: Having an Unclear Property Investment Strategy

At the point when asked by anybody how to put resources into property, I react with a progression of inquiries:

- What are your money related points? At the end of the day what are you after? Is it true that you are looking for a salary, capital or both?

There is a major contrast between needing to resign in 2 years so you can live off your investment salary and needing to assist your youngsters with educational cost costs in 12 years.

- Will you have to acquire cash and what amount of hazard would you say you will take?
- Will you think about contributing abroad, and assuming this is, where will you contribute - Europe, the Far East or the Middle East.
- What level of hazard would you say you will take?
- What occurs in the event that you need your cash back rapidly?

Keep in mind, liquidity is a noteworthy issue in property investment. In the event that you put resources into the stocks and offer market, you can get the telephone and sell in minutes. That is liquidity. Simply have a go at doing that with property and you'll see that it's a totally unique story.

- What about your assessment risk and what might occur in the event that everything turned out badly?
- Do you need to put resources into business or private? Do you by any chance know the distinction?

These are the sort of inquiries you ought to present yourself before you make a plunge and put resources into property. It's exceptionally useful to record your explanations behind needing to put resources into property. You can generally reconsider your rundown on the off chance that you alter your perspective on your investment intentions. In any case, I promise you won't be upset for investing a little energy in advance making the rundown. Then again, in case you can't concoct any inspiring components for contributing, you're likewise setting yourself up for disappointment. This may appear to be a great deal of work, however it's a significant piece of the procedure on the off chance that you need to succeed. Keep in mind: purchasing property BEGINS with an all-around idea out arrangement for your leave procedure!

You ought to likewise know about the serious promoting publicity of numerous online estate operator destinations; they regularly go after simple, ignorant people. Be mindful so as not to fall for the promotion with respect to the off arrangement arrangements advertised in almost every nation. Media, for example, lustrous abroad magazines that publicize second homes available to be purchased as investments are frequently deceptive.

Another expression of alert - don't be tricked or conned by the guarantees of "make easy money" property plans. Property is a long haul investment. It's anything but difficult to dismiss this as you hear any number of various, new and potentially all the more energizing property investment techniques that give off an impression of being profiting NOW. A long time back you could buy sensibly evaluated property, lease it out and take in substantial income in a moderately brief timeframe. Be that as it may, circumstances are different and this is not true anymore.

Not all real estate operators will be forthright about this reality. In the same way as other others, you may erroneously expect that your real estate operator is resolved to enable you to get the most ideal return for your cash. Tragically, this is frequently not the situation. The fundamental objective of real estate operators is to sell property - period. Do you think it is to their greatest advantage to persuade you to make long haul property investments? Certainly not!

Media assets can likewise hamper your property investment openings by composing terrible or great reports about property investments that essentially aren't valid. Property-related columnists are being paid to compose, not to lead inquire about the real estate showcase or rewarding investment openings. Publicizing is enormous business and columnists might be paid to compose a scorching or shining report about different abroad or neighborhood investments that is totally false. Thus, it's ideal to disregard most of what you read in the magazines and direct some strong statistical surveying alone. All things considered, it's your cash so you need to contribute it astutely!

Luckily, there are some solid assets accessible to enable you to find out about current patterns in the property showcase.

Likewise make certain to converse with nearby real estate operators just as some dependable rental management organizations. They can talk about a portion of the more fruitful nearby investment property methodologies. Remember about individuals from your neighborhood business network and retailers in your locale. They can demonstrate to be priceless wellsprings of data with regards to neighborhood property investment.

If you set up clear investment targets, you can concentrate just on the applicable kinds of property. I don't prescribe picking in excess of two property types in case you're an unpracticed property investor. Given the huge measure of conceivable investment properties, this little advance can spare you a great deal of squandered hours. You ought as far as possible the urban communities you're thinking about to a couple. You would then be able to decide the best and most exceedingly awful investment territories of a particular city by dissecting different factors, for example, wrongdoing and business measurements.

The main concern is don't depend on just the most recent investment prevailing fashions to figure out where to contribute your cash. This can demonstrate to be an expensive error, particularly on the off chance that you are new to property investment. Invest some energy deciding your rousing elements for contributing, ask yourself a few significant inquiries and tight your objective territory to a couple of urban communities. These means will significantly improve your opportunity of accomplishment. With a touch of arranging and exhortation, you can build up a reasonable investment procedure and maintain a strategic distance from the most widely recognized property investment botch.

The most effective method to Begin a Real Estate Business: With Little or No Money

The real estate part is a flourishing one. Many make investments; purchasing terrains and building houses to be set up for rent. Obviously, the most ideal approach to be a piece of it is to have cash for buys. Notwithstanding, you can at present purchase properties without having money. In spite of the fact that without cash, something still should be advertised. It could be your time, your ability, or your range of abilities. Indeed, there are bargains that should be possible without you having cash. How?

Accomplice

In the event that you have enormous thoughts, solid field-tested strategy and an incredible reputation, at that point you can get an accomplice who has what you don't – cash. The individual can give the financing while you remain on the overseeing part of the business. You ought to likewise talk about how benefits will be shared. Make it a success win for your accomplices and get it going.

Another type of joining forces is by contributing with a structure temporary worker. On the off chance that you do not have a few abilities, for example, carpentry and pipes aptitudes, to fix up and exchange a property, you can join forces with somebody who has these abilities and could help with the initial installment. When you make a benefit on the deal, you will have the upfront installment for your next real estate investment.

Converse with individuals
There is no cash expected to get it under contract or finding bargains for investors. You can help individuals discover bargains, at that point you can have individuals who will subsidize your arrangement, or even better, you may have bit by bit made cash to purchase your own property.

Get cash from family or companions
On the off chance that you have no cash to begin your real estate business, obtaining cash from family and companions is another alternative that you can utilize. This might be less formal, however make certain to give them an authority promissory note with installment due dates, a particular financing cost, and what ownership, assuming any, the moneylender will have on the property. Keeping your assertion is significant for it might decide how they will get you in the event that you have a comparative need later on. In the event that you pay back the credit on schedule and with intrigue, these loan specialists may be eager to loan to you again for future tasks. This is an extraordinary choice, yet numerous connections have been pulverized on the grounds that they didn't deal with the procedures included appropriately.

Work out an exchange
You can pay for real estate by giving the required/particular ability you have. For instance, a temporary worker could offer a real estate designer work in return for an upfront installment.

Search for frantic merchants
These individuals are frantic to sell for reasons, for example, insolvency, separate, the demise of a relative, an away new position, poor state of the property and so on. They are

generally all the more ready to give financing to make it all work out rapidly.

Investigate vender financing
On the off chance that the vender is inspired enough, they might be happy to make it simple for you to buy by giving you an advance. You could offer to make higher regularly scheduled installments rather than an initial installment. You could likewise arrange an arrangement where the dealer pays your upfront installment to the purchaser so as to sell the property quicker. The merchant may anticipate that you should pay him/her back or s/he may toss the upfront installment in for nothing, basically bringing down the selling cost.

Whatever you choose to do, ensure you get a real estate lawyer to review the understanding with the goal that the two gatherings are secured.

CHAPTER II
HOW RBRRR WORKS

Putting resources into Real Estate: The Simple Strategies

Purchasing and owning real estate is an energizing investment procedure that can be both fulfilling and worthwhile. Not at all like stock and bond investors, planned real estate owners can utilize influence to purchase a property by paying a segment of the all-out expense in advance, at that point satisfying the parity, in addition to enthusiasm, after some time. While a conventional home loan by and large requires a 20% to 25% up front installment, sometimes, a 5% initial installment is everything necessary to buy a whole property. This capacity to control the advantage the minute papers are marked encourages both real estate flippers and landowners, who can thus take out second contracts on their homes so as to make initial installments on extra properties.

Here are four manners by which investors can put properties to great use:

1. **Wanting to be a Landlord**

   Perfect for: People with DIY and redesign aptitudes, who have the tolerance to oversee inhabitants. The stuff to Get Started: Substantial capital expected to back direct upkeep expenses and spread empty months.

   Merits: Rental properties can give ordinary pay, while expanding accessible capital through influence. Also, many related costs are charge deductible, and any misfortunes can balance gains in different investments.

   Demerits: Unless you contract a property management organization, rental properties will in general be filled with consistent migraines. In most pessimistic scenario situations, unruly inhabitants can harm property. Besides, in certain rental market atmospheres, a landowner should either suffer opportunities or charge less lease so as to cover costs until things pivot. On the other side, when the home loan has been satisfied totally, most of the lease turns into all benefit.

   Obviously, rental salary is anything but a proprietor's sole core interest. In a perfect circumstance, a property increases in value through the span of the home loan, leaving the landowner with a more significant resource than he began with.

2. **Real Estate Investment Groups**

   Perfect for: People who need to claim rental real estate without the problems of running it.

   The stuff to Get Started: A capital pad and access to financing.

Merits: This is a considerably more distant way to deal with real estate that still gives pay and appreciation.

Demerits: There is an opening danger with real estate investment gatherings, regardless of whether it's spread over the gathering, or whether it's owner explicit. Moreover, management overhead can eat into returns.

Real estate investment gatherings resemble little common supports that put resources into rental properties. In a commonplace real estate investment gathering, an organization purchases or constructs a lot of loft squares or apartment suites, at that point enable investors to buy them through the organization, along these lines joining the gathering. A solitary investor can possess one or numerous units of independent living space, yet the organization working the investment bunch on the whole deals with the majority of the units, taking care of upkeep, publicizing opportunities and meeting inhabitants. In return for leading these management assignments, the organization takes a level of the month to month lease.

A standard real estate investment gathering lease is in the investor's name, and the majority of the units pool a part of the lease to make preparations for intermittent opportunities. To this end, you'll get some pay regardless of whether your unit is vacant. For whatever length of time that the opening rate for the pooled units doesn't spike excessively high, there ought to be sufficient to take care of expenses.

While these gatherings are hypothetically protected approaches to put into real estate, they are powerless against similar expenses that frequent the shared store industry. Besides, these gatherings are here and there private investments where deceitful management groups bilk investors out of their cash. Demanding due perseverance is in this way basic to sourcing the best chances.

3. **Real Estate Trading**

   Perfect for: People with noteworthy involvement in real estate valuation and advertising.

   The stuff to Get Started: Capital and the capacity to do or administer fixes as required.

   Merits: Real estate exchanging has a shorter timespan during which capital and exertion are tied up in a property. In any case, contingent upon economic situations, there can be huge returns, even in shorter time allotments.

   Demerits: Real estate exchanging requires a more profound market information matched with karma. Hot markets can cool out of the blue, leaving transient merchants with misfortunes or long haul cerebral pains.

   Real estate exchanging is the wild side of real estate investment. Similarly as informal investors are an alternate creature from purchase and-hold investors, real estate merchants are particular from purchase and-lease landowners. A valid example: real estate merchants regularly look to beneficially sell the underestimated properties they purchase, in only three to four months. Unadulterated property flippers regularly don't put resources into improving properties. In this manner investment should as of now have the characteristic worth expected to turn a benefit with no adjustments, or they'll kill the property from dispute.

   Flippers who can't quickly empty a property may end up in a difficult situation, since they ordinarily don't keep enough uncertain money close by to pay the home loan on a property, over the long haul. This can prompt kept snowballing misfortunes. There is an entire other sort of flipper who makes cash by purchasing sensibly estimated properties and including an incentive by remodeling them. This can be a more drawn out term investment, where investors can just stand to take on each or two properties in turn.

4. **Real Estate Investment Trusts (REITs)**

Perfect for: Investors who need portfolio presentation to real estate without a customary real estate exchange.

The stuff to Get Started: Investment capital.

Merits: REITs are basically profit paying stocks whose center property contain business real estate properties with long haul, money delivering leases.
Demerits: REITs are basically stocks, so the influence related with customary rental real estate does not have any significant bearing.

A REIT is made when a company (or trust) utilizes investors' cash to buy and work salary properties. REITs are purchased and sold on the real trades, similar to some other stock. A partnership must compensation out 90% of its assessable benefits as profits so as to keep up its REIT status. By doing this, REITs abstain from making good on corporate salary regulatory expense, while a customary organization would be saddled on its benefits and afterward need to choose whether or not to appropriate its after-charge benefits as profits.

Like ordinary profit paying stocks, REITs are a strong investment for securities exchange investors who want customary pay. In contrast with the previously mentioned sorts of real estate investment, REITs bear the cost of investors' entrée into nonresidential investments, for example, shopping centers or places of business, which are commonly not achievable for individual investors to buy legitimately. All the more significantly, REITs are profoundly fluid since they are trade exchanged. As it were, you won't require a realtor and a title move to enable you to money out your investment. By and by, REITs are a progressively formalized adaptation of a real estate investment gathering.

At long last, when taking a gander at REITs, investors ought to recognize value REITs that possess structures, and home loan REITs that give financing to real estate and fiddle with home loan supported protections (MBS). Both offer introduction to real estate, however the idea of the presentation is unique. A value REIT is progressively customary, in that it speaks to ownership in real estate, while the home loan REITs center around the pay from home loan financing of real estate.

Regardless of whether real estate investors utilize their properties to produce rental pay, or to wait for their chance until the ideal selling opportunity emerges, it's possible to work out a hearty investment program by paying a generally little piece of a property's all out an incentive in advance. In any case, likewise with any investment, there is benefit and potential inside real estate, regardless of whether the general market is up or down.

Tips for Diversifying Your Portfolio

At the point when the market is blasting, it appears to be practically difficult to sell a stock for any sum not exactly the cost at which you got it. But since we can never make sure of what the market will do at any minute, we can't overlook the significance of a well-differentiated portfolio in any economic situation.

For setting up a putting methodology that tempers potential misfortunes in a bear advertise, the investment network lectures something very similar the real estate market lectures for purchasing a house: "area, area, area." Simply put, you should never place your eggs in a single container. Which is the place broadening comes in.

What Is Diversification?

Broadening is a call to war for some, budgetary organizers, subsidize supervisors, and individual investors the same. It is a management procedure that mixes various investments in a solitary portfolio. The thought behind expansion is that an assortment of investments will yield a higher return. It likewise recommends that investors will face lower hazard by putting resources into various vehicles.

Figure out how to Practice Disciplined Investing

Expansion is certifiably not another idea. With the advantage of knowing the past, we can kick back and investigate the gyrations and responses of the business sectors as they staggered during the dotcom crash and again during the Great Recession.

We ought to recall that contributing is an artistic expression, not an automatic response, so an opportunity to practice trained contributing with an enhanced portfolio is before expansion turns into a need. When a normal investor "responds" to the market, 80% of the harm is as of now done. Here, more than most places, a great offense is your best safeguard, and a well-enhanced portfolio joined with an investment skyline more than five years can climate generally storms.

Here are five hints for helping you with expansion:

1. Spread the Riches

Values can be magnificent, yet don't place the majority of your cash in one stock or one part. Consider making your very own virtual common store by putting resources into a bunch of organizations you know, trust and even use in your everyday life.

In any case, stocks aren't only the main interesting point. You can likewise put resources into items, trade exchanged assets (ETFs), and real estate investment trusts (REITs). What's more, don't simply adhere to your own command post. Think past it and go worldwide. Along these lines, you'll spread your hazard around, which can prompt greater prizes. Individuals will contend that putting resources into what you realize will leave the normal investor also vigorously retail-arranged, yet knowing an organization, or utilizing its products and enterprises, can be a solid and healthy way to deal with this segment.

All things considered, don't fall into the snare of going excessively far. Ensure you hold yourself to a portfolio that is sensible. There's no sense in putting resources into 100 distinct vehicles when you really don't have opportunity or assets to keep up. Attempt to restrict yourself to around 20 to 30 distinct investments.

2. Consider Index or Bond Funds

You might need to consider including list reserves or fixed-pay assets to the blend. Putting resources into protections that track different records makes a superb long haul broadening investment for your portfolio. By including some fixed-pay arrangements, you are further supporting your portfolio against market instability and vulnerability. These assets attempt to coordinate the exhibition of expansive records, so as opposed to putting resources into a particular area, they attempt to mirror the security market's worth.

These assets are frequently accompanied low charges, which is another reward. It implies more cash in your pocket. The management and working expenses are negligible in view of the stuff to run these assets.

3. Continue Building Your Portfolio

Include to your investments a normal premise. In the event that you have $10,000 to contribute, use dollar-cost averaging. This methodology is utilized to help smooth out the pinnacles and valleys made by market instability. The thought behind this technique is to chop down your investment chance by contributing a similar measure of cash over some stretch of time.

With dollar-cost averaging, you put cash all the time into a predetermined arrangement of protections. Utilizing this system, you'll purchase more offers when costs are low, and less when costs are high.

4. **Realize When to Get Out**

   Purchasing and holding and dollar-cost averaging are sound procedures. Be that as it may, in light of the fact that you have your investments on autopilot doesn't mean you ought to overlook the powers at work.

   Remain current with your investments and remain side by side of any adjustments in by and large economic situations. You'll need to realize what is befalling the organizations you put resources into. Thusly, you'll additionally have the option to advise when it's an ideal opportunity to cut your misfortunes, sell and proceed onward to your next investment.

5. **Watch out for Commissions**

   In the event that you are not the exchanging type, comprehend what you are getting for the expenses you are paying. A few firms charge a month to month expense, while others charge value-based expenses. These can include and wear down your primary concern.

   Know about what you are paying and what you are getting for it. Keep in mind, the least expensive decision isn't generally the best. Keep yourself refreshed on whether there are any progressions to your expenses.

Uses of RBRRR Strategy

The current monetary conditions have made way for exceptional investment openings and furthermore some difficult snags for both the new and experienced Investor. All together for you as a Real Estate Investor to make long haul money related progress, you should execute powerful Risk Mitigation methodologies. The accompanying data will give you procedures you ought to consider as you are assessing potential investment areas and getting and overseeing investment properties.

Perhaps the greatest test Investors face today is verifying financing - You should comprehend the Lenders Underwriting criteria before going into the arrangement. With endorsing rules proceeding to turn out to be progressively prohibitive, you should investigate innovative approaches to get around customary financing. A portion of these strategies incorporate the accompanying:

- Other People's Money (OPM)
- Seller's Financing Hard Money
- Private Money
- Self-Directed IRA's from you or different Investors
- Joint Ventures
- Partnerships

It is extraordinary to persuade the Seller or a Hard Money Lender to subsidize the arrangement, yet do you have a leave procedure on how you will change from this transient financing? Having the property balanced out during your leave system execution will be basic to verify long haul financing from ordinary Lenders.

o **Being ready to change yourself in changing occasions** - What worked a year ago or even a month ago may not work today. For instance, when you glance back at Real Estate Agents and how they worked together in 2006 generally, purchasers would swarm to them and as a rule of an estimated right property, there was a free for all of offers that may have brought about offering up the business cost. In the present market, with couple of purchasers pulling the trigger or qualified for financing, the fruitful Agent must have a powerful promoting arrangement to draw in the purchasers in the market. Many have experienced issues with this change and are never again ready to continue themselves in the business.

- **Development of a far-reaching Business Plan** - Your Business Plan is your guide that will lead you towards your investment objectives. Generally, numerous individuals either don't have a Business Plan or are not utilizing it as the useful asset it may be. Coming up next are some basic components of an effectively actualized Business Plan, effective objective setting should meet the accompanying "Shrewd" attributes:

  - Specific
  - Measurable
  - Attainable
  - Relevant
  - Time bound

> High level objectives must stream down to what you ought to chip away at every day. This is a zone where numerous individuals experience difficulty and therefore, get disheartened in accomplishing their objectives.

> The Business Plan is a living archive that ought to develop with you.

> Your duty to work your Business Plan is fundamental.

> Understand your dangers and relieve whatever number of them as would be prudent

> The present market isn't excusing and on the off chance that you settle on a terrible choice or things go somewhat off track, it could be the part of the bargain.

- Put a solid expert group set up
- Use them in your everyday business choices; not exactly when it is the ideal opportunity for charges or your need them to audit a deal.
- Have the correct group. Ensure you are utilizing experts who really know your business. I hear so often that individuals are utilizing an inappropriate experts in their group. Because your Uncle is an Attorney does not mean they have the contributing background that will profit you. Keep in mind when choosing your group, you are talking with them!
- Develop a viable system to help guarantee your long haul achievement
- Attend investment association occasions. This gives the inspiration numerous individuals need.
- Come to the gatherings early and remain late; this is the place you will get the chance to "work the room".
- Meet whatever number individuals as could be expected under the circumstances and trade business cards. It will be crucial for you to catch up with these contacts so as to begin to set up an association with them. Keep in mind, every individual you meet has their own system that at last you may access. This is a region I feel numerous individuals battle with. This isn't about what number of business cards you gather and put in a shoebox, it's tied in with creating connections.
- Don't confine your systems administration just to real estate gatherings. There are numerous associations that could profit you as a Real Estate Investor.
- Prepare yourself with a strong investment instructive establishment - Only through information would you be able to get hazard and how to moderate hazard.

- ➢ Have a strong resource assurance plan set up - Here is another region numerous Investors miss the mark. In these belligerent occasions, you should set up defensive measures so somebody doesn't go along and remove all you have developed.
- ➢ Be appropriately safeguarded - Make sure the property use is meets the strategy. Continuously consider the most elevated risk inclusion accessible.

What is the least hazard plan of action to make long haul riches and income that will support advertise variances? The Hold to rent plan of action is an incredible decision; when you consider the gratefulness, income, standard decrease, charge impetuses, and the capacity to use your capital, it is clear why probably the best investors are intensely into this model.

Top of the List Risk Mitigations

1. **Don't utilize the highest point of the market rents when assessing properties** - If the property bodes well at 90%, you have a champ. No one can really tell when you may need to limit the lease dependent on an evolving request.

2. **Calculate execution on the most traditionalist use** - If for instance you are concentrating on understudy lodging which normally makes more pay than a solitary family rental, utilize the lower single-family number. I have seen an excessive number of Investors buying properties dependent on the understudy lodging model just to find that they couldn't find intrigued understudies and therefore, went topsy-turvy with the property.

3. **Never consider unlawful condos and the pay it produces when assessing investment choices** - One call to the town from a furious neighbor or inhabitant and you are in a major upset potential fines and the evacuation of the illicit loft and occupants. Additionally remember, when you are thinking about illicit use and inhabitance, you are in risk if a protection guarantee is ever documented. Your insurance agency will probably decline to cover the case and that can have an overwhelming effect in the event that somebody gets injured.

4. **Use traditionalist inhabitance desires** - Never utilize the present zone inhabitance rate when assessing investments. On the off chance that the property is as yet an entertainer 5-10% beneath the present inhabitance midpoints of the region, you will have an edge to ride out any interest shifts.

5. **Has great income** - Make sure you are getting adequate income in your properties with the end goal for it to support itself monetarily. The exact opposite thing you need is to need to go into your pockets every month to cover costs. On the off chance that for instance, one empty month costs expends the positive salary you will make throughout the following 4 months, you are putting yourself at incredible monetary hazard. We see today unreasonably numerous associations offering total bundle bargains at what is by all accounts incredible section costs just to discover that toward the part of the bargain you are left with $150! I'm certain you know how effectively that can get retained in the event that you needed to get an exchange contractual worker for a normal fix.

6. **Have great overall revenues in a Wholesale or Flip arrangement** - In a solid Seller's market, you can have littler edges when doing a Wholesale or Flip. In any case, during a Buyer's market, bigger edges will be required so as to ensure yourself in the event that you have to limit the business cost.

7. **Have a solid value position going into an arrangement** - Having a solid value position when obtaining a property will enable you to use this value by hauling out capital for some time later. What's more, it will give you a support in the occasion the market brings a down-turn.

8. **Have satisfactory capital stores** - I see such a large number of Investors utilizing all their accessible cash-flow to buy the property and to place it in administration without building up any stores. These stores might be vital because of the accompanying circumstances:
    - Hold you over during the rent up period
    - Expected fixes
    - Unexpected fixes
    - Budget over-runs
    - Utility cost development

9. **Take time to become more acquainted with the individuals you plan on working with** - Developing a strong association with the individuals you plan on working with is so significant. Things can turn out badly with business connections from numerous points of view that incorporate the accompanying:
    - People who are deliberately out to exploit you

- People with great intensions yet maybe not fit for conveying on their guarantees

It will be significant that before you engage with anybody at any degree of business that you lead the proper degree of Due Diligence that incorporates performing foundation and reference checks. Keep in mind, the media ceaselessly helps us to remember the extortion that happens in business and you must do everything conceivable to abstain from becoming involved with it.

10. **Always have a leave technique** - As a parallel to what they show you in protective driving courses, you ought to consistently have an out of your investments particularly if things begin to turn out badly. Successful leave procedures ought to be considered during the assessment and securing stages. For instance, how about we accept your investment technique was to buy a property with the goals of flipping it. Imagine a scenario in which the market began to chill off real quick, having a Hold to rent methodology arranged just in the event that you couldn't draw off the Flip would be a powerful leave technique.

11. **Know your investment territory like a master** - As an Investor; it will be significant for you to have exhaustive information of your focused on investment region. Despite the fact that having neighborhood experts to help you in finding, obtaining, and dealing with the properties is an extraordinary asset, you ought to never depend exclusively on them to figure out what a feasible investment opportunity is. Give yourself some an opportunity to become more acquainted with your

focused on region and what a shouting arrangement resembles. With this understanding, you will almost certainly pull the trigger immediately which is generally required on the best of the arrangements.

12. **Always assess the investment with property management charges included** - Even on the off chance that you plan on dealing with the property yourself, it is astute to include the fitting property management expenses; this will cover you in the occasion you are never again ready to self-deal with the property.

13. **Have a decent comprehension of the four market cycles** - Each market cycle accompanies diverse investment systems. When you become capable in distinguishing the market pointers, you will have more control on the most proficient method to deal with your portfolio and investment choices.

CHAPTER III
HOW TO DETERMINE A GOOD RENTAL PROPERTY

Rental real estate is gradually turning into a wise investment attempt despite the fact that there are some distrustful rare sorts of people who still believes that it's an overwhelming endeavor. Well we can't accuse them since scanning for a wise investment property is really hard. In any case, for those couple of positive *thinkers* rental property is incredible approach to aggregate riches.

Much the same as a business undertaking it is significant that you have a solid arrangement or procedure on how you will build up your rental real estate into a lucrative undertaking. Else, you will wind up losing the majority of your investment. You have to do some meticulous research and most likely have a few associations with locate a gainful rental property. This is on the grounds that your goal is to make benefit inside the most limited time conceivable. This is additionally a similar motivation behind why you should discover a vender that is eager to give you free value.

Here are a few hints to enable you to begin with your rental real estate business:

1. You need an investment plan since this will enable you to decide the length of your ownership of specific rental property. Keep in mind that the more you claim the property, the more you'll spend on upkeep, fixes and upgrades. On the off chance that you need to make any real enhancements for the property, make certain the deal cost will be sufficient to take care of the expense. In the

event that you don't know, at that point better not spend excessively. In any case, owning the rental estate property for less time would likewise make greater investment hazard particularly when purchasing in an overheated market. To make up for that hazard, you need a greater potential yearly return. For some little investors, be that as it may, long haul ownership is keen since it permits them a lot of time to outlive any vacillations in the market - and furthermore since the rental salary can be a decent beneficial pay meanwhile. Being a landowner is even a remunerating day work for a few.

2. There are different methods for discovering properties and these are as per the following: chase properties that are now for abandonment, you will almost certainly get some data by methods for become a close acquaintance with city corridor assistants or bank workers who know about properties that are going to be dispossessed or are as of now abandoned; you may likewise attempt to contact a real estate operator who's vigilant for conceivable purchases; or you may join a neighborhood proprietor or property owner's relationship with the goal for you to make contacts. And keeping in mind that you're grinding away why not ask proprietors straightforwardly to check whether they are ready to selling; you may take a stab at looking in papers for rental advertisements or you may drive around neighborhoods so as to scan "for lease" signs.

Get your funds fit as a fiddle

In the event that you really need to take part in a rental estate property business you need a decent credit standing - which means less Visa obligation and other purchaser obligation. Lenders more often than not require greater up front installments, charge higher loan costs and need your funds to be fit as a fiddle when you are purchasing rental properties.

It really pays to have a huge money hold in the wake of purchasing any property since there may be some required fixes that rental property may require. In the event that you can bear to put aside in any event one month lease for every unit, which is a decent start. You may likewise attempt to apply for a credit extension verified either by the property or your very own home so as to take care of bigger expenses.

Abstain from overspending

The motivation behind why you contribute on a rental estate property is for you to pick up benefits and not to lose each sparing you have. Ensure that despite everything you have spare enough for your retirement before putting resources into rental real estate since simply like any business wherein you will in general lose a few and afterward win some yet just to err on the side of caution attempt to spare as much as you could. Should be set up than be sorry later on.

Registration a Rental Property: Type of Property Desired

The main choice that you have to make is the sort of property that you need to put resources into. A great many people pick single family homes to begin since they are most acquainted with that sort of real estate. Condos, apartment suites, duplexes, and business property are for the most part reasonable sorts of rentals. Today, with the present condition of real estate, singular single family homes are getting the most consideration. Numerous people are leasing instead of buying because of vulnerability in the economy. This has brought about rents being higher than ordinary; a circumstance that ought to be considered before purchasing rental property.

Locate a Real Estate Agent

Select a Real Estate specialist that you can work with. Examine the sort of Real Estate you might want to put resources into and the value run. Disclose to the specialist that you will think about dispossessions and furthermore property that is recorded by the present owner. It is key that you set aside the effort to guarantee that the specialist comprehends that you are an investor and won't live in the property; your objective is full-time rental and income. The operator is roused by discovering you a property to put resources into, which is the way he/she profits. You can anticipate that the real estate operator should disclose to you why the property will fit in with your craving to purchase a decent rental property.

Do Your Own Research

Research for the money saving advantages of the property ought to be finished by you. Decide the standard, intrigue, charges and home protection costs. This will require gauges for cost and loan cost that the real estate operator can assist you with. A traditionalist methodology is utilize the approaching cost as the reason for cost. To decide rental value I like to add 30% to the entirety of these expenses to cover opening and fixes; utilize an assumption that is agreeable for you. Give this data to your real estate specialist; no sense in taking a gander at properties where the asking cost is drives the rental cost out of thought. Find in any event three properties that fit your valuing criteria; this will enable you to move between the three properties during arrangement.

Arranging the deal

The exchange will be with an owner or on account of dispossessed property the bank. Consulting with a mortgage holder is typically progressively troublesome because of the way that value development influences the owner legitimately. With a dispossession exchange have the real estate specialist set up the gathering. The examination done above to decide rental cost will be comprehended and increased in value by an investor. On the off chance that the bank is asking an excessive amount of it is anything but difficult to demonstrate that the property won't income. Keep in mind, the bank has a non-performing resource that is costing cash for support, power, protection, and insurance from vandalism; they are roused to sell at a sensible cost.

Thought Questions for Purchasing a Rental Property

A proprietor is just as fruitful as his property will enable him to be. In the event that you don't have a decent rental property or you overpaid for your property, you'll have a troublesome time discovering accomplishment as a landowner. Picking a rental property is the most significant choice you'll make, so you must be sure beyond a shadow of a doubt that you've placed in the examination to enable you to go to the correct choice.

When choosing a rental property, there are a few inquiries you have to consider:

> ➤ **Can I bear the cost of the upfront installment?** Numerous moneylenders see rental property as a higher hazard, and accordingly, they frequently request a greater up front installment on the credit. Here and there, they could request that you put down as much as 40% on the property. Converse with your bank to decide the amount you'll need to put down, and in the event that you can't realistically manage the cost of it, you'll have to think about another property to put resources into.

> ➤ **Will the market rental worth spread the home loan?** This comes down to basic arithmetic and Being a Landlord 101. Your rental rate needs to cover the home loan. In case you're paying more every month than you're acquiring, you're not going to make a benefit as a landowner (except if you're additionally living on the property). On the off chance that the rental rate you need is to cover the home loan isn't in accordance with the market esteem, you shouldn't make the investment.

- **Is the structure appropriate for leasing?** There are sure codes that structures need to meet before they can be leased lawfully. Acclimate yourself with the leasing laws in your general vicinity, and have the structure examined by an expert to make certain everything is up to code. On the off chance that it's not up to code, you need to factor in the expenses of improving the structure to get it up to code. This is a significant advance, so ensure you don't skip it.

- **Will any fixes or redesigns should be made?** Don't simply take a gander at the sticker price on the property as it stands. You need to likewise consider any extra cash you'll have to place into the investment for updates. This could be anything from as little as changing the locks to as large as gutting the spot and remaking the internal parts. You need to consider each cost so you can decide whether it genuinely is a savvy investment.

- **Is the property situated in a protected and secure zone?** Wellbeing and security are constantly top worries for leaseholders, especially on the off chance that they have youngsters. On the off chance that the property itself doesn't appear to be secure or it's in an especially hazardous neighborhood, you're most likely going to experience serious difficulties leasing it out and seeing an arrival on your investment. Look online for audits on neighborhood security, check wrongdoing insights, and take a drive around the region during the evening. Ensure there is a lot of lighting, and change/add locks to the entryways and windows.

Be endlessly careful when making an investment in rental property.

Step by step instructions to know a Good Rental Property

There are four principle factors that show whether a rental property is a decent bargain: the pay it creates, the area, the accessible financing and the honest estimation of the property with respect to the price tag. In this article, we will see how to investigate a rental property in one of these zones - assessing a properties salary - to know whether you are really getting a lot.

Stage One: Analyzing Cash Flow

After acquiring some basic data from the dealer, you can sort out and dissect that data to decide the measure of positive or negative income an imminent property will deliver. Try to utilize yearly numbers as opposed to month to month when finishing your income investigation.

Give us a chance to survey the Property Cash Flow Analysis:

> ➤ *Gross Income:* In this area of the Cash Flow Analysis, an investor includes the planned or anticipated rents and all other anticipated that salary should decide the Gross Scheduled Income (GSI). He at that point subtracts the opportunity stipend or anticipated opening, taken from the present opportunity rate for the zone, to land at the Gross Effective Income (GEI).

> ➤ *Expenses:* Here, the investor decides the all-out Operating Expenses (OE) by including every one of

the costs engaged with the activity of the property excluding any obligation administration.

- ➤ **Net Operating Income:** The Net Operating Income (NOI) is the contrast between the Gross Effective Income and the Operating Expenses.

- ➤ **Debt Service:** Debt Service (DS) is the complete head and intrigue installments for every one of the home loans or credits used to secure the property.

- ➤ **Cash Flow:** The property's Cash Flow or Net Income (NI) is the Net Operating Income less the complete Debt Service (DS). This can be a positive or negative number.

Stage Two: Verifying the Numbers

In some cases to get a higher price tag, a vender will blow up the measure of salary a property produces or basically neglect to specify the majority of the costs really required to keep up the property. Regularly the vender will be totally fair with the data he supplies, yet some significant makes sense of are accidentally left. For instance, this could occur if the merchant deals with the property himself and does exclude a property management expense in the numbers he gives you. The merchant might not have stayed aware of essential fixes and upkeep on the property, in which case the costs he supplies may not be adequate for you to sufficiently keep up the property. Shockingly, if the purchaser puts together his idea with respect to wrong data, he could lose a great deal of cash. As the purchaser, you should shield yourself from this by confirming the majority of the data you get on a property. You should take the data you get from the dealer daintily until you have confirmed its exactness.

There are various approaches to check a property's salary and costs:

1. ***Property Operating Statements:*** These announcements are regularly alluded to as Profit and Loss or Income and Expense proclamations. A decent investor will track all the pay and costs delivered by his property on a month to month and yearly premise. You can look at the data furnished by these announcements with the data that the dealer at first gave. It is a smart thought to get the property's Operating Statements for in any event the previous three entire years just as year-to-date. Be careful about adulterated data. Numerous merchants and realtors will dishonestly publicize a property's Operating Statements by furnishing a planned purchaser with a Pro-forma. A Pro-forma does not take its numbers from what the property really created, yet rather gives their gauge of what the property should deliver. The overall gain appeared by these assessments are quite often definitely higher than what the property is really creating. The vender or realtor will endeavor to legitimize the evaluated numbers over the genuine numbers by proposing that the present rents are low, or if some minor fixes are done the property's estimation would increment. Regardless of what their reasons are, your offer ought to be gotten from the numbers that the property is right now creating. In the event that you can build its incentive through lease expands, fixes or whatever it might be, the advantage ought to be yours and not for the seller.

2. ***Schedule E(s):*** A Schedule E is the government tax document that reports real estate pay and costs. The property's addition or misfortune as appeared on this

structure is then added to the owner's other salary to decide his government annual assessment commitment. Timetable Es will give the most exact bookkeeping of a property's salary and costs. This is in such a case that the merchant has forgotten about costs that he has paid on his property, at that point his assessment commitment will be higher. Since nobody needs to make good on additional in regulatory obligations, they remember to incorporate any of the appropriate costs. A merchant may admit that he included a bigger number of costs or recorded less pay than there really was so as to bring down his duty commitment. Regardless of what is asserted, you need just pass by what is set up on the Schedule E. In the event that the dealer lied on his government forms, at that point a lower price tag for his property might be the outcome. Try not to go out on a limb by going on somebody's promise alone.

There are costs that are some of the time excluded on the Schedule E that you should include when investigating a property's pay: property management, yard support, and snow evacuation. There are additionally a few costs on the Schedule E that you can prohibit: devaluation, intrigue, dinners and diversion, and travel. In looking into the Schedule Es, demand duplicates of at any rate the previous three years. Be careful with proceeded with exceptional decreases in rental salary over these years. This could demonstrate a negative change in the market or the region's economy. On the off chance that there is such a decay, attempt to decide its motivation so you can all the more astutely continue with or end the investigation procedure.

Not all investors utilize a 1040 Form Schedule E to report their real estate salary. On the off chance that they claim their property in an organization, at that point they won't utilize this structure. If so, despite everything you need to investigate a similar data that would be accounted for on a Schedule E. You can do this by mentioning from the dealer duplicates of all government forms identifying with the property and social event the data from them.

3. *Utility Companies:* By calling the service organizations, you can discover the property's careful utility cost history.

4. *County Tax Assessor's Office:* The Assessor's office has on record all property charge commitments, just as any unpaid property charges.

5. *Lease Agreements:* By looking into the present leases, you will know the careful measure of lease that the property right now creates.

6. *Market Rents:* Even however a property might be as of now getting a specific sum in rents, it is as yet conceivable that these rents are not honest rents. On the off chance that a property is leased anomalous higher than the equitable rates, another purchaser will battle to get them leased for a similar sum when the present leases lapse. Acclimate yourself with current market leases so you can make the suitable changes in accordance with your offer.

7. *Insurance Company:* Insurance rates will fluctuate from customer to customer and friends to organization. Along these lines, you can't expect that your protection rate for a property will be actually equivalent to the current owner's; nonetheless, they are normally genuinely close. Call around and value rates from various organizations to locate the best one for you. Make a point to think about comparable plans. In the event that the inclusion being offered isn't the equivalent, at that point the rates will be extraordinary. You have to analyze rates for a similar

inclusion. Ensure that the organization you pick has aggressive rates, but on the other hand is an outstanding, legitimate organization.

The most effective method to Determine If a Multifamily Property Is a Good Investment

There are a few different ways that you measure how fruitful a particular multifamily property investment is probably going to be. You could take a gander at the rental development rates and the opening inhabitance rates to decide how well a specific rental property is doing at present, yet these numbers won't demonstrate to you how well this particular property will perform later on. You could likewise decide to just buy multifamily real estate properties in the beach front markets, or the business sectors that are as of now creating a great deal of ROI. This nonetheless, will make them contend with each other investor in the nation for properties that may not be worth what you will pay for them or fundamentally produce long haul gains later on. You would prefer not to just see things like inhabitance rates, rental development rates or how appealing the area of the property is on the off chance that you need to precisely check the investment estimation of the property. To really decide whether a specific multifamily investment property merits your time take a gander at the best 4 parts of a top business rental investment. In fifth spot underneath, some last tips before you pull the trigger on your new investment.

1. Great Population Growth

The best places to find great multifamily investment properties are areas that show exceptionally solid developments in populace. There are not many things that produce enthusiasm for rental properties like a detonating populace. Areas that have a critical inundation of new inhabitants are the best places to purchase business real estate. The explanation for an area's populace blast is an interesting point in any case. The best areas are ones that are picking up populace through relocation or the formation of new families. Spots where new individuals are joining existing families are not as valuable to the business property investor.

2. Occupants Who Are Young and Mobile

Areas with more noteworthy quantities of youthful and versatile occupants are better for rental property owners, as more youthful individuals will in general lease homes more than they get them.

3. Areas with Expanding Employers

At the point when a huge organization extends its business base, increasingly youthful and versatile inhabitants move into that area. This makes the business rental properties around there progressively significant to investors. Savvy investors put their cash into business sectors that show solid rising patterns in bosses and employment development. Search for areas with better than expected development in work, or areas where enormous businesses are opening for business. Chances are these huge organizations will acquire a ton of new inhabitants, who will all need a loft to lease.

4. Explicit Submarkets

Most business lodging investors search for business sectors that are either delegated high obstruction, implying that it is hard to locate a rental loft for the leaseholder (think New York City) or markets that are anything but difficult to locate a rental property (like Texas). Be that as it may, on the off chance that you set aside the effort to locate a quite certain submarket in a simple to get into territory, you could discover the big stake for business real estate here. For instance, most pieces of Texas are anything but difficult to locate a rental condo, with the exception of a not many areas that are viewed as recently grew top of the line markets. These high boundary areas in simple market territories make great business real estate investment decisions.

5. Property by Property Analysis

When you have limited your investment down to explicit submarkets you have to weigh out various investment properties inside that region. Here a specialist with involvement in property management and ownership is your most solid option for finding incredible multifamily investment properties. Try not to think the leaflets you get from operators contain anything besides the rosiest forecasts. Get somebody who can really endorse your investment for what it will do, or as near it as could be expected under the circumstances. This isn't only a scientific endeavor dependent on salary, expressed costs, obligation administration, and different expenses. You need somebody to do the majority of this inside the structure of cautious property due steadiness and information of market points of interest where property management is concerned. You need somebody who will factor in your important capital enhancements, cautiously survey occupant data, and different issues that may come up during a property examination. Two "indistinguishable" structures beside one another on a similar road may perform diversely relying upon how they have been overseen before, the inhabitant base, owner relations with neighbors and nearby experts, etc. The factors are many. Ensure you get the most experienced financier and property management individual you can to speak to you.

CHAPTER IV
HOW TO DETERMINE WHAT TYPE OF RENTAL TO BUY

Rental properties can be amazingly gainful in any economy. The focal points ought to be self-evident. To give some examples, month to month income, gratefulness in incentive for a long haul investment, and with the vulnerability of the economy and individuals losing their home to abandonments numerous new properties are available at a diminished rate and a lot more individuals are going to leasing as the main alternative.

When you are thinking about rentals as a possibility for your portfolio presently is a perfect time to do as such. Outfitted with the correct learning of how to prevail with rentals you can situated to benefit from the current monetary condition. Actually you can do so fiercely and getting to be well off all the while. Envision repeating month to month salary from stable long haul occupants.

What is required is the eagerness to go out on a limb associated with acquiring any property for a rental. Obviously it must be an educated hazard and it must be vital as far as area and where you will locate the most ideal leaseholders and where your property estimation will increment. This may take some time and exertion to investigate however there are numerous open doors where a key money related choice including great sound judgment can be made.

Numerous individuals are hesitant to purchase any properties right now because of all the dread and vulnerability encompassing our economy. Others are looking for the open door that exists because of the new conditions that have surfaced in light of the lodging business sector breakdown. In the event that you are one of the ones who are frightful or dubious the best counsel I could offer is to look carefully and in detail at the upsides of rental properties.

When you have concluded that you are need to profit by the income and income of rental properties there are three explicit ways that you can make your properties incredibly beneficial:

1.) **Quality management:** The more you can think about the properties and put resources into their upkeep, with both the present moment and long haul at the top of the priority list the more beneficial they will turn into. A few owners concede upkeep to not far off and shockingly it thinks about the nature of the management and the long haul estimation of the property.

2.) **Location and Quality of Tenants:** Depending on where the rental property is found will decide the nature of leaseholders and the value that can be charged per tenant. Clearly the objective is to have long haul tenants paying a premium for a quality rental. This will augment your arrival on investment and increment your income month to month.

3.) **Attention to Tenant Retention:** To keep your occupants they basically should be seen as your benefits and along these lines treating them and their needs and demands with the most astounding need. Numerous property owners disregard their inhabitants and don't serve them or their needs. This will just prompt high opportunity rates which will affect your month to month income among different issues.

You can augment your pay and month to month income through rental properties with practically zero cerebral pain. Right now is an ideal opportunity to start to learn, research and start the way toward doing the math so as to settle on educated choices about the most ideal areas and properties to gain.

Instructions to Buy Investment Rental Property

With the cost of houses dropping you might consider how to purchase investment rental property as a benefit making system. The objective is to discover reasonable real estate that you can rapidly lease to occupants. The contrast between what you pay on home loan and upkeep and what the rental pay ought to be a decent positive income.

Putting resources into rental property delivers practically easy revenue, which implies that once everything is set up, the benefits come in predictably on a month to month premise. Sometimes there will be time and additionally cash required in the upkeep of the property. Due determination in exploring the property and the state of house will give you a smart thought of what fixes should be made en route.

I feel compelled to pressure this progression as much as possible. Ensure you set aside the effort to get the property assessed to maintain a strategic distance from huge forthright support charges... check whether the property as of now has a rental history... also, get some information about the exhibition of rentals in the territory you are looking.

In the event that you are new to putting resources into rental property there is a decent possibility you don't really realize where to start. Here are a couple of pointers to begin:

- Figure out your investment spending plan and how you will fund the upfront installment. This is an entire article in itself, however I can reveal to you that banks are searching for a 20% up front installment
- Do some examination on fixed rate and variable rate contracts
- Get your home loan agent to prequalify you for the buy
- Decide the area where you need to possess rental properties
- Contact a nearby realtor's office and converse with a realtor who has some expertise in the purchasing and selling of investment properties
- Join a system of different people who are specialists at putting resources into real estate. They can enable you to decide a decent area to purchase rental properties and answer some other inquiries you may have. There are a few decent online informal organizations for real estate investors also.

Putting resources into real estate can give you a feasible wellspring of positive salary on the off chance that you are eager to place in the exploration required to settle on a wise investment choice. You can discover progressively about how to purchase investment rental property that is in a top notch area for tenants by asking at your nearby realtor's office or joining a system of different investors.

Properties of Rental Investment: Time to Buy or Sell

How can one decide when to sell a rental property investment? On the off chance that you are going to purchase rental properties - having an arrangement set up for the fitting time to sell is significant.

I have worked with numerous people throughout the years and told them the best way to purchase rental property. There are numerous things that should be viewed as when acquiring for investment purposes. There is additionally - certainly - an opportunity to sell.

Step by step instructions to Buy an Investment Property

- **Is the property in a helpful area?** Is it close to shopping, in an area with great schools, and is it effectively available to interstates and associating streets?

- **Does the potential investment property have a sound establishment?** What kind of issues does the home have? In the event that it needs another rooftop or the establishment is depressed in and is making issues inside the structure, it probably won't be a wise investment right now. In the event that the issues are just corrective (needs another washroom floor, or painting, or covering) it might be advantageous. Examination reports will uncover the property's defects so the purchaser and real estate expert can settle on a decent choice.

- **Do you have a sufficient up front installment to buy the rental property so financing won't be an issue?** In the present real estate showcase, most loan specialists will see an upfront installment of 40-half as a decent hazard. In the event that you can put 100% into the property - this is shockingly better.

- Income picked up from the property needs to surpass costs. Distinguish a credit commendable occupant, a dependable property director, and a strong rent to make your property investment gainful. Property management expenses are charge deductible.

- For private property investments, single-family homes just as multi-inhabitant properties, for example, duplexes and fourplexes are incredible approaches to manufacture pay and riches. A few investors might need to consider high rises. For this situation a business property advance will be important to get financing.

- Use devaluation on the investment property as an approach to get a yearly charge finding. Check with your bookkeeper, who will apply the deterioration finding on the structure, apparatuses - even window medications. The administration still permits charge conclusions for quickened devaluation on properties. Sharp real estate investors utilize this conclusion to build income and net working benefit on a property.

At the point when to sell a Rental Property

I have a term for properties that should be sold: gator properties. These are properties that are eating the investor buzzing with conveying costs. At the point when an investor takes a gander at the main concern on a croc property - there is no benefit - just costs. A croc property today may have been a wise investment ten years back. However, a few people will keep on holding a property until it drains the majority of the benefits they may have made in the initial 5-7 years.

On the off chance that a property has nostalgic worth (it was your first home, or your mom once claimed it yet now she's expired), a few investors may will in general need to clutch it. Having an enthusiastic connection to an investment property that should create salary isn't great. Some of the time an individual will hold this sort of property regardless of whether it isn't productive. It might be a great opportunity to think about selling this property.

- After a specific number of years, the deterioration charge finding is spent on a property. Ask your bookkeeper when this deterioration is never again relevant. At the point when the investment can never again be deteriorated - it's an ideal opportunity to sell that property, and buy another rental.

- Consider selling the property and applying the 1031 duty code, so no capital additions assessment is forced on the benefits. To summarize, the code expresses that an owner can sell one property in return for a securitized bit of property or occupant in like manner bit of property. Fold the benefits from one property into another investment to build riches and look after it.

- By and large, in the twelfth year of property ownership - the time has come to sell an investment. The choice to sell will rely upon two elements. 1. Is there enough value in the property to sell? Or then again, have you hauled out an excessive amount of value in the property? 2. Will the real estate market enable you to sell and get a decent benefit? Approach a real estate proficient for a custom market examination on the property to check whether it's realistic to get a value that nets a pleasant benefit.

- **Alligator properties are not productive for an assortment of reasons.** I am astounded at the quantity of investors who are not in any case mindful that their property is losing cash. In the event that you have a property that may lose cash, at that point ask your real estate expert or bookkeeper to play out an expense to pay investigation. On the off chance that it is in fact a crocodile property - think about selling.

Investors purchase and sell values constantly. There is an opportunity to buy and an opportunity to sell a home too.

Ten Buying Tips for Rental Properties

Purchasing rental properties is a decent method to build your advantages. Be that as it may, picking the correct rental property will challenge. Here are a couple of things to check for preceding purchasing rental property.

1. **Area** - Most individuals would prefer not to live in the shelter docks. The area of your rental property will decide how simple it will be to lease. In the event that you have a ton of vehicle traffic, you may get a more noteworthy reaction from a sign at the area than you will from a paper include.

   Occupants need to live in pleasant neighborhoods near every one of the comforts. They need to be near the schools, stores, recreational areas, medical clinics, and work. I haven't met any individual who needs to live in a bothersome neighborhood or drive 15 minutes for a gallon of milk.

2. **Numbers** - When purchasing rental property you need to check the numbers. Ensure you have every one of the costs related with that property and ensure despite everything it has a positive income. Contemplate the

upkeep issues, any utilities not secured by inhabitant and amortize the expense of the huge activities like heater substitution, new material, siding or finishing.

These tasks just happen once every 15-20 years however you might come in to this in the tenth year of that cycle. Make sure to compute your costs high and your salary low. This can spare you a few astonishments not far off. Anticipate that the unit should be vacant in any event one month out of every year because of turn over. You should repaint and clean the rugs the initial 2 weeks, at that point promote and demonstrate the following 2 weeks. You should just rely on 11 months of lease for every year.

3. **Lower Maintenance Buildings** - You need to keep away from homes that will require costly routine support. A few models would be homes that have cedar-shake shingles or siding, wood sided structures, wood outline windows, block garages, cedar decks, and so forth.

Attempt to look not far off and decide the future support needs. Keep in mind the lower the upkeep the less migraines and bigger benefits.

4. **Higher Home Prices** - Check in towns with higher home costs, since this expands the interest for rental property. Search for the monstrous house on the square that has a lower cost, empowering you to buy inside the edges.
After some inside and outside paint, somewhat light finishing and new drapes, viola', a house that will get premium lease as a result of the class of neighborhood. On the off chance that individuals can't stand to purchase

a home in this class they should lease. This will make an interest for rental property.

5. **Beneath Market Rent costs** - When purchasing rental property, search for rental property which has lease costs that are underneath ebb and flow market rents. This will enable you to raise the lease and increment the estimation of the property. According to over, this may simply require a little cushion to empower raising the rental cost.

   Rental property market worth is controlled by the measure of pay gotten by the rental property. Anyway remember, if the rental property has leaseholders when you buy it, they dislike it when you raise the lease. Additionally verify what kind of rent is set up. The rent goes with the deal. In the event that the present tenant is paying an unsatisfactory cost and has 1/2 years left on the rent it could end up being a losing recommendation.

   There is just a single method to stop a rent as another owner. You should redesign the spot. Check with the nearby lodging commission to perceive what the base cost prerequisites of redesigning are for quick expulsion of current rent holders.

6. **Great Rental History** - Whenever purchasing rental properties, you should check the rental history. Verify overall to what extent inhabitants are staying and do they pay their lease on schedule. A few neighborhoods are normally snappy turnover times. Close to air terminals, uproarious bars or clubs, close to army installations, and so forth.

7. **Agrees to Zoning and Fire Codes** - Make sure you verify whether there are reviews required by nearby authorities for rental properties and does this property pass those assessments. You never know the real reason the present owner is selling the property.

   It might require broad fixes to pass the investigations. A brisk warning would be if the power has been killed for more than 90 days. They will as a rule require a review before reestablishing power, particularly in the event that it is a known rental.

8. **Under Twenty Years Old** - This is clear as crystal, in the event that you confine your choice to structures that are under twenty years of age, you will constrain the odds that the structure will have any construction regulation or upkeep issues. The structure could be close to the upkeep cycle for rooftop, paint and potentially heater yet the structure will be sound and not requiring redesigned windows, siding or concrete fix.

9. **Out of State Owners or Managers** - When purchasing rental property, search for properties that are claimed by out of state owners. It is difficult to oversee rental property from out of state and when these come available to be purchased, the owners are normally more worried about selling rapidly than getting as much as possible.

   So as to lease a spot rapidly you should live close by so you can demonstrate it at the guest's solicitation. As a rule they will request to see it in the following 20 minutes or thereabouts. Take into account their solicitations and show it snappy. Most tenants need a spot inside the following week or something like that and won't hold on to see your place until one week from now since you are occupied.

Most occasions they will settle on a choice before tomorrow when it would be progressively advantageous for you to indicate it. This has transpire too ordinarily. Never give out the location for drive-by. Forthcoming leaseholders will request the location to do a drive by and simply take a gander at the spot. Try not to burn through your time with these people. Demand demonstrating it in the following 30 minutes or you won't give out the location as a graciousness to the neighbors.

10. **Neighborhood is steady or improving** - clearly maintain a strategic distance from neighborhoods that are declining, take a gander at the composition on the dividers and remain out. In spite of the fact that these may look great because of the low price tag, they are hard to gather the rents.

    By discovering neighborhoods that are steady or improving, it will be simpler to lease the property and you will almost certainly expand the lease. The general accord is, the better the area the higher the price tag and the higher the lease costs, in this way the edge for benefit is more noteworthy. The less fortunate the area the lower the price tag and lower the lease costs decreasing the overall revenues.

CHAPTER V
HOW TO FIND LOW COST PROPERTIES

HOW ANALYZE THEM TO MAKE SURE YOU ARE CHOOSING THE RIGHT PROPERTY

What is the best alternative for your money investment? Generally safe investments that give an exceptional yield on investment, obviously! That is the reason such a significant number of effective investors go to real estate putting resources into rental properties.

Be that as it may, shouldn't something be said about the majority of the frightfulness stories you've caught wind of real estate investors losing huge amounts of cash from rental properties? They're most likely racing into your brain as you hear "Purchasing rental property is perhaps the best choice for okay investments."

The reason these accounts exist? Each choice a real estate investor makes when purchasing rental property influences whether it will be an okay money investment or not. In this way, if a real estate investor does not adapt precisely how to discover generally safe investments when purchasing rental property, his/her real estate investment can come up short.
In any case, rental properties can be the best generally safe investments.

For what reason Are Rental Properties the Best Low Risk Investments?

Before figuring out how to discover okay investments when purchasing rental property, realize you're settling on the correct decision for your money investment. Investigate why rental properties are the best generally safe investments.

Investment Properties Generate Monthly Rental Income

When purchasing rental property is done well, a real estate investor can begin making positive income from rental salary inside the main month or something like that. No other generally safe investments enable the investor to begin making cash back on a money investment so rapidly without selling.

Investment Properties Are Tangible Income Producing Assets

The watchword here is "substantial". In the wake of purchasing rental property and checking the accomplishment through positive money flow (or scarcity in that department), a real estate investor can make a move and influence change. Having the option to control the accomplishment of a money investment makes rental properties generally safe investments.

Investment Properties Appreciate in Value

Other than profiting from rental pay, the estimation of investment properties will in general go up. Particularly in the present lodging market, which is a seasonally tight advertise all around, gratefulness will in general occur at a quicker rate. This implies selling these okay investments quite often ensures an exceptional yield on investment.

Steps to Finding Low Risk Investments When Buying Rental Property

We presently realize that rental properties can be generally safe investments, yet there are sure stages a real estate investor can take to guarantee he/she finds an okay real estate investment.

Step #1:

Location in the Real Estate Market
The initial step is pinpointing the best places to put resources into real estate for generally safe investments. An area in the real estate market can influence everything about okay investments: their capacity to pull in inhabitants, cause rental salary, to create positive income, and sell for a decent rate of return. There are two sections to this progression when purchasing rental property: picking a city with a promising real estate market and finding the best neighborhood for investment properties.

The Ideal Real Estate Market for Low Risk Investments
A real estate showcase with the best places to put resources into real estate will above all else have a sound economy that displays work development. Search for a real estate advertise that has new rising organizations or effective organizations that are growing or moving to the city. This will prompt populace development and an expanding interest for investment properties.

A real estate investor should investigate joblessness paces of an area just as the enhancement of the business. An area subject to one industry could mean awful things for real estate contributing if that industry falls or migrates.

The real estate showcase you pick when purchasing rental property can really represent the deciding moment the arrival on investment. Search at an area with minimal effort to lease proportion for the best okay investments. A decent degree of profitability comes when a real estate investor can charge a decent lease value contrasted with the price tag of the investment property.

The Ideal Neighborhood for Low Risk Investments
Picking the best places to put resources into real estate doesn't stop at finding an incredible real estate advertise. The decision of neighborhood for investment properties is similarly as significant, as the real estate contributing potential can differ from neighborhood to neighborhood. In the event that you need a simple method for picking the best places to put resources into real estate, investigate the area to guarantee it advantageously has walkability and access to open transportation, low wrongdoing rates, and great school locale to guarantee investment properties will be generally safe investments in that area.

Step #2:

The Condition of Investment Properties
When a real estate investor has discovered the absolute best places to put resources into real estate, it's an ideal opportunity to pick a genuine investment property. Perform investment property examination to choose which investment property will be a standout amongst other generally safe investments.

Investment property examination will help a real estate investor decide whether the state of the rental property will help in getting a decent rate of profitability or hurt its odds. The best generally safe investments in real estate don't require an excessive number of fixes, yet still, have some space for constrained appreciation. An investment property with restorative fixes like a requirement for new paint, covering, or another apparatus or two is a sheltered decision for your money investment.

A home review ought to uncover what fixes are required. Investment properties with major auxiliary issues, rooftop harm, or water and electrical framework harm won't make for okay investments.

Investment property investigation, just as home review, ought to uncover the age of the investment property, which a real estate investor needs to contemplate when purchasing rental property. Why? The more established the investment property, the more upkeep and fixes it will require. Regardless of whether the home investigation uncovers no requirement for fixes now, an old investment property will require them soon later on.

Here is the manner by which to think about the ages of an investment property and the fixes required:

- 5-10 years of age: practically no upkeep
- 10-20 years of age: more upkeep
- 20-30 years of age: will require substantially more fix: rooftop, water warmer, funneling, and so forth.

Make certain to check the home review report; more seasoned rental properties that have had a profound redesign as of late can at present be generally safe investments.

Step #3:

Return on Investment

A system that guarantees generally safety of investments is real estate contributing for positive income. On the off chance that a real estate investment has positive income from the beginning, a real estate investor will profit when an inhabitant is set up to give rental pay.

Positive income is the point at which the yearly rental pay of an investment property surpasses the majority of the costs required to claim and look after it (fixes, charges contract, and so forth.). Proceeding with investment property examination, a real estate investor must complete computations to decide whether there will be sure income for an exceptional yield on investment.

The best rate of profitability metric to use for investment property investigation is money on money return:

Money on Cash Return = (Cash Flow/Cash Invested) x 100

With a positive income, the money on money return estimation will demonstrate a positive rate of profitability. Real estate specialists concur that any investment property which can give 8% or higher will expedite a decent return investment and positive income.

Step #4:

Exit Strategy
The last advance in discovering generally safe investments in the real estate market is ensuring a leave technique is set up before purchasing rental property. There are two principle leave procedures in real estate contributing:

- Buy and hold (long haul or present moment)
- Selling the investment property

Either leave methodology ought to apply to generally safe investments effectively: one as the leave procedure to utilize quickly and the different as a reinforcement leave system, on the off chance that things don't go as arranged.

Rental properties can be generally safe investments for profiting in real estate. A real estate investor simply needs to make the correct strides when purchasing a rental property. Concentrate the area, the state of the investment property, and the arrival on investment, and plan for a leave technique.

Great Rental Property Choosing Tactics
What would it be a good idea for me to search for in an investment property? This is a typical inquiry for real estate investors. Figuring out how to decide a decent rental property will mean the distinction between a gainful investment and a terrible investment.

There are various elements that go into deciding whether a rental property is a wise investment. This article will disclose when to purchase dependent on market cycles, where to purchase, what kind of investment property to purchase, and what a decent return on an investment property is.

At the point when to Buy Rental Property
Understanding business sector cycles will enable you to choose when to purchase. To do this, you should almost certainly perceive if the zone you're taking a gander at is an economically tight advertise or a wide open market.

As we are hoping to purchase an extraordinary rental property, we need to purchase during a fast moving business sector. A fast moving business sector is when there are numerous homes available and not a ton of purchaser's – giving purchaser's everything the power. Purchase during a fast moving business sector. Sell during an economically tight showcase.

Where to Buy Rental Property
Much the same as the climate, real estate is very area subordinate. The real estate market can be hot in one town and cold in the following. Indeed, even inside a similar city, you can have more than one real estate showcase. The area of a property is commonly viewed as the absolute most significant factor in deciding its worth.

You need to search for a property in a decent neighborhood, in a decent school area, near employments and nearby pleasantries. These components will probably build the estimation of your rental after some time – as long as these variables remain the equivalent.

The most effective method to Spot Good Locations

There are incredible markets everywhere throughout the nation. In each state, you can discover pockets of business sectors on the precarious edge of development. Here is a portion of the criteria we search for:

- Is it situated close to a major city? Enormous urban communities can extend employment opportunity expansion, alongside culture, nightlife, and helpful comforts.

- How enormous is the populace and is it developing? Hope to put resources into urban communities with more than 1 million occupants. In many zones, around 40% of the populace rents, which leaves 400,000 potential occupants for your rental property.

- You don't need to purchase a property in a major city. The key is to take a gander at a whole metro zone to decide the best neighborhoods. You may find that there is really a more noteworthy interest to purchase in suburbia of a major city, where the wrongdoing rates are lower, schools are better and the enhancements are more pleasant. Try not to purchase excessively far away from the city as individuals for the most part would prefer not to live over 30 minutes away.

- Is it in a decent advertise? Investors can decide whether the territory is encountering a purchaser's or economically tight showcase by checking stock levels and to what extent it takes for a property to sell (normal number of days on market, or DOM).

- Are home costs expanding or diminishing every month? A decent general guideline is to see home estimation drifts over a continuous multi month time span.

- Is there rental interest? Sites and neighborhood property supervisors can give data about rental interest in the region.

- Does the zone have a low middle or normal home cost? Middle home costs are essentially the widely appealing properties. In a moderate market, the normal home cost ought to be close to 3 to multiple times the normal pay.

What Type of Rental Property Should I Buy?

There are various approaches to profit in real estate. You may put resources into a business property, mechanical property, a whole high rise or a solitary family home.

Whatever you choose is the best course for you, pick one, gain proficiency with the intricate details, stick to it and become a specialist. You can't do everything, in the event that you need to do it well. Pick the system that works for you and put your vitality into that by itself.

The single-family home is the least difficult approach to begin as another real estate investor. Furthermore, numerous master investors will reveal to you it's the absolute best investment in real estate. From our experience, the best kind of single-family homes have in any event 3 rooms and 2 showers.

When you consider what you search for in a home for your family, odds are it's a solitary family home and not a duplex, triplex, townhouse or condo. Single-family homes are much simpler to both lease and sell than multi-family homes.

In the event that you are attempting to sell a multi-unit property, no doubt different investors will hope to get it. As we understand, investors are continually searching for an arrangement and would prefer not to pay the maximum. While single-family homes can be offered to people in general at retail cost. On the off chance that your property is reasonable to the normal purchaser, you ought to hope to have a lot of interest when you sell or lease.

This is particularly obvious when you've set aside the effort to purchase a decent rental property. Where it's situated in a decent neighborhood, with great schools, near occupations and access to nearby luxuries.

More reasons we like to put resources into single-family homes:

- Easier to upkeep
- Higher quality inhabitants
- Faster appreciation
- Easier Financing
- Affordable value focuses

Instructions to Analyze Investment Properties

When you're out taking a gander at potential investment properties, it's essential to realize how to break down them. Accepting you've pursued our tips on where to get, you at that point need to run the numbers. This incorporates the anticipated lease and thankfulness and every one of the expenses or costs related. Remember to incorporate, shutting costs, escrow expenses, charges, potential opportunity and home loan expenses.

While there might be a great deal of costs, make sure to consider month to month lease, energy about the property, yearly increment in lease and tax cuts you fit the bill for. Each and every time you take a gander at a home, make a point to utilize your income investigation condition and let the numbers represent themselves.

After you've separated every one of the numbers, you would then be able to choose if this rental is going to accommodate your investment procedure and produce positive income.

To recap, here's the manner by which to decide a decent rental property:

- Located in an alluring territory close to occupations
- Ideally in a metro zone with more than 1 million individuals
- Single-family homes
- Well-kept up and refreshed
- Priced in the middle range for the zone
- Priced between $100,000 to $200,000

What is a Good Return on Investment Property?

Contingent upon who you ask, anything over a 15% ROI could be viewed as a decent return on a real estate investment. Be that as it may, there are a couple of approaches to precisely ascertain your potential rate of return.

Ascertaining ROI

The arrival on investment (ROI) is a measure used to assess the proficiency or benefit of an investment. As it were, the measure of return with respect to the investment's expense.

Return on initial capital investment = Annual rental salary/Total money investment

Computing Capitalization Rate

The capitalization rate or top rate, is the pace of profit for a salary property dependent on the net operating income (NOI). The top rate demonstrates the pace of return considering your strategy for financing. Investors for the most part consider a decent top rate above 8%, and particularly 10%.

Top rate = NOI/Price

Computing Cash on Cash Return

A money on money return or COC return, measures the yearly return on your investment dependent on the NOI and the all out money investment. Your COC changes relying upon various financing techniques. By and large, a great COC return is above 8%, yet go for above 10% or 12%.

COC Return = NOI/Total money investment

In contrast to the financial exchange, real estate is simpler to foresee, on the off chance that you realize what to search for. To remain over market cycles in the zone your rental is found, you have to focus on any changes.

Essentially go on the web and search for school evaluations, nearby bosses, wrongdoing rates, rental rates, home rates and populace shifts. In the event that you notice negative things occurring around there, you can generally choose to offer your rental property before qualities start to diminish and purchase in a best in class neighborhood.

CHAPTER VI
HOW TO FINANCE RENTALS

The mystery in real estate business is to utilize other individuals' cash. This is the way most real estate big shots are made. Not at all like customary private real estate contracts, real estate financing offers a lot more extensive money related choices, including loaning or financing from different monetary foundations. Exchanges like these call for better than expected arrangement abilities.

It's not prudent to put your very own cash in a real estate concerning a couple of significant reasons. To begin with, you will in general give a large portion of your benefits away by not utilizing your investment. Second, real estate is an extremely dangerous business - you would prefer not to imperil all that you have.

It is not necessarily the case that real estate investment is about misfortunes. Despite what might be expected. On the off chance that you realize how to make cash work for you, you may really gather a lot of cash as a byproduct of your investment.

Here's the secret:

On the off chance that you buy a $100,000 property that expands a normal of 7 percent for each year (in reality that number could be higher or lower), you would see a net benefit from leasing your property bringing about a roughly 15 percent return.

In case you're content with little return of investment, you may settle with your 15 percent return. Be that as it may, on the off chance that you really need to acquire on your investment, think about what utilizing can accomplish for you. At present, a common real estate investor can discover financing as high as 95 to 97 percent of the price tag. There even a few occasions where you might probably get a 100 percent financing yet we won't utilize this for our model as it's a deficient correlation.

Along these lines, in case you're are an investor who is as of now content with a small return of investment then 15 percent seems like a great deal. Be that as it may, for the individuals who really need to become wildly successful in the real estate, 15 percent is a long way from being viewed as a vital return.

How does utilizing work?

How about we expect that the rental pay will cover every one of your costs, including the home loan installments. Taking a similar model, a 7 percent valuation for your property brings about a $7,000 benefit for each year. With a 95% financing set up, you'll have the option to get a $7,000 return on $5,000 (your 5 percent initial installment on a $100,000 real estate property). This will furnish you with a 140 percent return on your investment. Not just that, with the equivalent $100,000 you can go out and buy 20 investment properties, money 95% percent of them, and make an astonishing $140,000 benefit a year. This thoroughly beats the $15,000 benefit with an all-money exchange.

Regarding the extra 20 properties, hope to experience considerable difficulties getting financing for them since generally just five or six new rental property home loans are the most extreme that moneylenders by and by permit.

Which is the reason you need a better than expected arrangement aptitudes.

Innovative Methods for Financing a Rental Property Purchase

The conventional way to purchasing an investment property is to set aside cash for an upfront installment, at that point get a home loan to cover the rest. In any case, that is by all account not the only way. Every once in a while, I get inquiries from the landowners who use Avail about how they can back a rental property in the event that they need more in the bank for an upfront installment.

Here are the four techniques proposed for thought.

1. Dealer Financing

This includes getting an advance from the individual you're purchasing the property from. At times, if the merchant is eager to loan you cash, it's simpler (read: less desk work) than getting an advance from a bank.

I've seen these arrangements work in various situations: The merchant may back either the initial installment or the full price tag. The merchant may be another property investor — or they may be the property's live-in owner.

The way to progress is to guarantee you concur on a reasonable financing cost for the advance. In the event that you don't have much involvement here, it might be shrewd to work with your CPA or potentially lawyer. What's more, paying little heed to how much encounter you have, make certain to get the provisions of the credit recorded as a hard copy, with marks.

2. Organizations

Another extraordinary financing choice is to collaborate with somebody who has enough cash for an initial installment. This is a compelling system on the off chance that you have a companion or relative who's keen on engaging in property investment, however perhaps isn't as intrigued by the everyday work of screening inhabitants and gathering rent installments.

In this situation, what frequently happens is that one accomplice sets up cash and different handles all the real work of being a proprietor. The way to progress here is to concede to how to part continues. I suggest considering it as far as adjusting the hazard and reward to expenses and advantages. Your accomplice is going out on a limb on all the budgetary hazard, however you're placing in all the legwork of acquiring income by means of lease. Ensure the manner in which you split continues mirrors your commitments.

Whatever you choose bodes well, it's ideal to have your terms recorded as a hard copy.

3. Government Programs

The Federal Housing Administration (FHA) was established to support homeownership. One of the manners in which it does that is by offering homebuyers the opportunity to purchase property with only 3.5% down.

While FHA advances are explicitly intended to encourage the buy of owner-involved homes, it's totally reasonable to purchase a two-, three-or four-unit building, live in one unit, and procure rental pay from the others. Truth be told, this can be an unbelievably savvy approach to back a rental property, particularly if it's your first.

FHA credit cutoff points are distinctive in each region, so part of the craftsmanship here is ensuring as far as possible where you need to purchase is sufficiently high that you can buy a multiunit property.

4. Retirement Accounts

Many individuals who have moved occupations every now and again or worked for themselves for any time allotment have retirement cash in an IRA. On the off chance that you have a self-coordinated IRA, you're permitted to put resources into nontraditional resources, which means an option that is other than stocks or shared assets. Real estate is an affirmed investment class, which means you can utilize cash in a self-guided IRA to back a rental property.

In the event that you go this course, however, chat with your CPA first. Indeed, even with programming that makes it simpler to be a landowner, real estate is an a bigger number of hands-on investment than anything in the financial exchange. Before you dive in, prepare sure you're to contribute the time and vitality important to see an advantageous degree of profitability.

Keep in mind; Pay Attention to Details

Notwithstanding how you fund your rental property, make sure you have sufficient desk work set up to set you up for progress and consistent pay from the property you purchase. That implies putting resources into:

• Formal (composed) concurrences with a dealer who has consented to loan you cash toward a property buy.

• Legal records like a LLC working consent to characterize who does what in an organization (and who gets what remuneration).

• Projections of expected comes back from different investment types from your monetary organizer so you can look at potential results.

Putting resources into real estate can be fulfilling and rewarding. To get the best advantage as long as possible, it's ideal to deal with the subtleties from the earliest starting point.

Financing Multiple Rental Properties

Purchasing various rental properties on the double is, to be sure, a rewarding endeavor, particularly on the off chance that you are hoping to develop your real estate investment portfolio rapidly. Not exclusively would it be able to enable you to develop your investment portfolio, yet this methodology will likewise give numerous salary streams every month. Things being what they are, the reason doesn't each apprentice real estate investor do this? Since they do not understand how to back various rental properties without a moment's delay. Indeed, the general concept appears to be outlandish for generally amateurs.

Presently, in spite of the fact that it is difficult, we have assembled a couple of alternatives that will unquestionably enable you to figure out how to fund various rental properties. Along these lines, right away, here we go!

One Loan, Multiple Rental Units

One approach to back various rental properties is to purchase numerous units in a single structure. A wide range of multi-family real estate fall inside this classification including condo structures just as duplexes and quadruplexes.

All in all, how can one fund various rental properties of this type?

You can apply for standard home loan credits at the neighborhood bank. It is like the home loan you would get the chance to purchase a house to live in, with a couple of additional necessities, obviously. Be that as it may, you should fire setting something aside for an initial installment for investment property route before you look for subsidizing. Ordinarily, it is a 20% initial installment. Be that as it may, you can at present discover contract loan specialists who will require less.

Financing Two to Four Rental Properties

How to back numerous rental properties when you're thinking about purchasing less than 5?

You can go to your neighborhood home loan representative or bank for investment property financing. For this number of rental properties, you need the accompanying:

1. A FICO assessment no under 630
2. An initial installment for investment property prepared
3. A quarter of a year of money holds for the ideal home loan installment

Be that as it may, one thing you have to remember is the sort of moneylender you go to. It's ideal to maintain a strategic distance from real banks. More often than not, such banks will in general be careful with the borrowers, so they require stricter criteria. Rather, work with nearby agents and search for banks which are typically more eager to fund under five rental properties.

Financing Five to Ten Rental Properties

For this number of rental properties, the bank will back your real estate investments if:

1. You have a FICO rating of 720
2. You have a half year worth of stores for assurance against opportunities
3. You have an upfront installment of 25% for single family homes and 30% for multi-family real estate properties
4. You don't have any history of dispossessions or chapter 11

5. You didn't fall behind on home loan installments (for your main living place) for the most recent year

Financing More Than Ten Rental Properties

For this measure of real estate investment advances, you need to go to significant loaning affiliations, for example, Bank of America. However, much the same as different choices, you should have your financial assessment prepared just as your upfront installment.

Is It Possible to Take Multiple Mortgages for Rental Properties?

Indeed, it is conceivable to take a few home loans on the double to fund numerous rental properties. Nonetheless, the quantity of home loans will rely upon your home loan moneylender and its confinements. Some will give you a chance to take the same number of as is allowed and others will restrict you dependent on your FICO assessment and capacity to cover installments. Along these lines, for this, you should perform appropriate due persistence.

Step by step instructions to persuade your home loan bank to back different rental properties for you

Most importantly, ensure you are prepared for the measure of desk work the loan specialist will be require. Your home loan moneylender ought to have the option to compute your obligation to-pay proportion which changes with each rental property investment you make. Thus, set up the entirety of your budget reports just as other money related information that the loan specialist requires. You will require these to affirm for your capacity to reimburse the home loan.

Second, incorporate beginning computations of the home loan in your marketable strategy. It must comprise of the measure of upfront installment you can give, the sum you anticipate that the moneylender should offer and the measure of regularly scheduled installment you can pay. You can utilize a home loan mini-computer for exact outcomes.

Prior to you even converse with a bank about how to back various rental properties, feel free to make sense of certain numbers. Figure all the arrival on investment measurements, for example, the income, the top rate and the money on money return for every one of the rental properties. You need high rates to persuade them all things considered. Additionally, examine the area and discover about thankfulness rates just as rental interest in that nearby showcase. At long last, set up everything together in a real estate marketable strategy and give it to your home loan banks.

How will you compute all that?

To play out a total and intensive rental property examination, you will require a rental property number cruncher. It will likewise fill in as a home loan number cruncher by considering how all the home loan information you accommodate it influences the ROI of a rental property.

Step by step instructions to Finance Multiple Rental Properties: Other Ways

Despite the quantity of rental properties you are attempting to subsidize, different techniques may require somewhat more from you. For instance, you can go with a sweeping home loan however be prepared to confront its dangers.

You can likewise go to hard cash banks. Be that as it may, likewise, be prepared to reimburse the home loan in a brief period. Else, you may be liable to abandonment.

CHAPTER VII
HOW TO REPAIR AND MAINTAIN PROPERTIES

Probably the greatest choice you will make as a proprietor is whether you should enlist a property management organization or not. Numerous landowners oversee properties all alone or with the assistance of a representative, for example, an inhabitant administrator. Once in a while it happens that proprietors need more help when property issues are confounded. This is when proprietors need to look for the assistance of real estate property management organizations.

Real estate property management organizations can be a colossal resource for your organization yet they don't come modest. They manage prospects and inhabitants, sparing you time and stress over advertising your rentals, gathering rent, dealing with support and fix issues, reacting to occupant objections, and notwithstanding seeking after expulsions. A decent property management organization brings its skill and experience to your property and gives you the significant serenity that accompanies realizing your investment is in great hands.

A real estate management business is a self-employed entity and this causes you stay away from the issues of being a business. Alongside the advantages, enlisting a real estate property management organization likewise accompanies a disadvantage of being a costly one. On the off chance that you are living a long way from your rental property, it will be hard for you to deal with property issues from a far distance. The vast majority of the landowners anticipate discovering great inhabitants to keep up their property in great and appealing condition.

In actuality, there are not many landowners who take a gander at their property absolutely as an investment and are not keen on loaning them to any occupants. For this situation, the best choice is to procure a real estate property management to deal with the property and deal with the related issues. Regardless of whether you appreciate hands-on management, you will come up short on time to focus on the development of your business which will place you in a circumstance to contract help for your property. Enlisting help of a real estate property management organization is an appealing choice on the off chance that you can bear the cost of the expenses for the equivalent. While talking with management organizations, hope to hear statements running somewhere in the range of 5% and 10% of what you gather in lease income.

A rental property won't appreciate long haul occupant maintenance and satisfactory degree of profitability except if it is kept up appropriately. This includes:

- Preventive and continuous upkeep;
- Repairs to address issues or breakdowns; and
- Construction and redesign

The Role and Responsibilities of a Rental Property Manager

Keeps up property rentals by promoting and filling opening; arranging and implementing leases; keeping up and verifying premises.

A property chief is an outsider who is contracted to deal with the day by day tasks of a real estate investment. They can deal with a wide range of properties, from single family homes to enormous high rises. Duties can be very expansive, including keeping up property rentals by filling opening, arranging and upholding leases, setting and gathering rent, screening forthcoming occupants, taking care of protests, keeping a precise spending plan and keeping up and verifying premises.

The property director is in the middle of the inhabitant and you, the owner. They are the "principal line of resistance" and they are there to secure you, to deal with all issues so effectively that furious inhabitants or specialist organizations are not calling you in the night.

As to and physical upkeep and fixes, a portion of the particular duties may include:

- Investigating and settling inhabitant grumblings; reviewing empty units and finishing fixes; arranging remodels; contracting with explicit upkeep administrations, for example, carpentry, plumbing, power, finishing and snow evacuation administrations
- Supervising fixes.
- Establishing and implementing preparatory strategies and techniques; reacting to crises.

Magnificent property chiefs are proactive and thorough.

Protection and Ongoing Maintenance

Preventive and progressing support of rental properties requires an exhaustive information of the property, its requirements for upkeep, staffing required to achieve the errands (or contracting with administration experts) and planning to achieve them. The real estate property director must adjust the expenses of standard and preventive upkeep with the advantages and wanted outcomes. Details on a property supervisor's normal support rundown may include:

- Cleaning of normal regions;
- Landscape upkeep;
- Regular administration to warming and cooling frameworks;
- Periodic examination of pipes and electrical things;
- Proper upkeep of wood, material and other structure parts.

Fixes (Repairs) and Corrective Actions
Repairs and corrective activities are required when things break or stop to work as proposed. At times the fix is of a crisis nature, for example, a warming breakdown in winter, while at different occasions these fixes can be booked and done productively in gatherings. It is the duty of the property director to know the distinction and to serve the requirements of the occupants while adjusting costs. It's additionally critical to deal with little issues before they become huge ones.

Development and Remodeling
Development and renovating are a piece of the office and building support. Redesign or development of the structure may be required:

- For exceptional business prerequisites of a business inhabitant;
- To right out of date quality of the structure; or

- To oblige uncommon physical needs of an inhabitant.

A real estate property supervisor can be extremely gifted at all different elements of management, however on the off chance that they fail with regards to office upkeep, the property will encounter a debasement of condition, loss of occupants, and declining rents.

Maintaining and Up-keeping a Real Estate Investment Property

We chat on and on about how you can possess a real estate investment property or how to put resources into real estate, yet what individuals frequently overlook is the significance of dealing with their real estate property. Like whatever else throughout everyday life, your real estate investment property needs uncommon consideration and fastidious consideration to be fruitful and remain effective. So by what means can real estate investors keep up their real estate investment property? What is required to keep up predictable inhabitance in their rental properties? Give us a chance to discover.

Owning a real estate investment property can be exceptionally useful and can turn into a fundamental hotspot for your pay. It accommodates numerous individuals' extraordinary income, leaving them with additional cash, even after every one of the bills have been paid. The individuals who claim real estate investment properties have the benefit of controlling their prosperity or their disappointment. They get the chance to control the circumstance and their money related future. Some portion of expanding your prosperity and advantages from your real estate investment property is figuring out how to look after it. There are numerous preferences to keeping your property slick and clean. An all-around kept up property would maintain worth and draws in better quality inhabitants, which advantages the two sides.

Tips and rules on the best way to keep up real estate investment property:

1. Investigate both the outside and inside of your rental property

Having your rental property well-kept and free from any harms will build your benefit and enable you to clutch great inhabitants. Unanticipated costs like fixes and substitutions are unavoidable when dealing with a rental property and you shouldn't put them off. Here is a rundown of things to search for when examining your rental property.

Outdoor

Roof: verify whether there are missing shingles, harmed blazing or shape and greenery. These can cause expensive harms later on. Additionally verify whether there are any tree appendages that expand onto your rooftop and cut them off. You need to abstain from having any of these since it very well may be a real side road for a large number.

Windows: verify whether every one of your windows are fixed appropriately without any holes and if there are holes, seal them. This will spare you spare you later on from dampness harm and warmth lost.

Exterior painting: ensure that the outside of your rental property is constantly painted so as to shield it from dampness and sun harm. No one needs to live in a house that looks terrible outwardly.

Landscape: check for broken tree limbs or trees with parasite. Anything that may carry mischief to your occupants, make sure to fix it. Likewise ensure the grass is sound and consistently cut it with the goal that any new occupants going by could see that your property is well-kept up.

Indoor

Water radiator: make a point to deplete and consistently expel any soil from the water warmers. On the off chance that you live in a territory with a great deal of silt in the water, you should seriously think about making this a month to month task.

Smoke indicators: this is certainly an absolute necessity. Continuously watch that your smoke alarms have new batteries and capacity appropriately. Living in a house with smoke alarms that don't work can be extremely hazardous.

Heating and cooling: you ought to consistently assess the warming and cooling framework. Check the channels and ensure there aren't any plants developing around them. This can limit the wind current and may destroy the framework later on.

Paint: check for any paint chippings or shape that may be on the dividers and consistently re-paint your dividers for a spotless and crisp inside.

2. Keep your inhabitants cheerful

One of different ways you can keep up your real estate investment property isn't by fixing harms in your property, yet additionally keeping your occupants fulfilled. Only a basic examination to perceive how things are going or inquiring as to whether they need anything will work.

Demonstrating to them that you are consistently there to help and that their fulfillment is your need will really have any kind of effect. This will help with your notoriety for future inhabitants and will draw in numerous individuals to your rental properties. React to their fix demands. One of the principle reasons inhabitants move out is on the grounds that they are upset, so make a point to keep your occupants satisfied.

3. Contract a property director

Dealing with your rental property can turn into a mind-boggling task. It requires some investment and necessities ordinary checkups. For the individuals who feel it's a lot of an over-burden, they can employ a property director that will keep up their real estate investment property. It is a major choice since these administrations are exorbitant, yet consider all the time you will spare. A property supervisor can do all that you need from inside to outside right to dealing with the month to month lease.

4. Adhere to the Landlord Occupant Law

Adhering to the proprietor occupant law will help you in keeping up your real estate investment property and help you in overseeing it accurately. It will give a structure to both you and the inhabitant in order to not commit numerous errors and keep your rental property in great condition. One of the commitments under the landowner law is upkeep so adhering to this law accurately will profit you a great deal.

5. Revamp and Improve

Inhabitants are continually looking for new and created rentals. As an owner, you ought to consistently consider approaches to revamp and improve your real estate investment property. For models, including another style of outside plan, such as overhauling the yard or including a nursery, or modernizing the inside by including frameless glass dividers. Do some exploration on new inside structures that are moderate. These better than ever changes will draw in inhabitants from everywhere.

Inhabitants reserve the privilege to appreciate a protected and tenable living condition and it's the homeowner's obligation to deal with and keep up the property. A well-kept property will help increment your prosperity and income. Continuously discover approaches to settle rental property issues before the issues get greater.

CHAPTER VIII
HOW TO RECRUIT TOP TALENT TO WORK ON YOUR PROPERTY

As a real estate pioneer or brand, your group is the most important resource you have. Having said that, how might you enroll the best real estate ability, and keep them?

1. **Adaptable work game plans:** Campaign Track suggests offering adaptable work courses of action. This may mean opportunity in adjusting in-available time from home hours. Adaptability can likewise apply to planning. Given your real estate colleagues convey the outcomes, does it really make a difference when they do or don't work?

2. **Proactively empower downtime:** Just on the grounds that your real estate group has adaptability in their calendar doesn't mean they will be compelling at utilizing it. There are a lot of real estate pioneers, CEOs, and investors that could be adhering to a four hour work week, yet wind up working 100 hour weeks, 52 weeks every year. In the event that you don't proactively help suit and advance ordinary downtime, you will lose individuals due to burnout. Tragically, as a general rule, it will be your best workers. Think about inciting, and notwithstanding paying them to take a break every year.

3. **Limits and advantages:** Real estate organizations shouldn't lose everything by offering such a large number of costly advantages, however they can offer a significant menu of limits. Outsider organizations and specialist organizations will regularly leave pocket for

the limits so as to enroll the business your real estate organization can offer. This can incorporate protection items, retirement plans and exercise center enrollments, autos, lodging, and shutting related administrations. A little can go far according to your representatives.

4. **Offers:** Real estate business visionaries with a foot in the startup world should as of now be well commonplace that giving offers is currently normally expected for key representatives and colleagues. In the event that you are really heading off to some place, offers can be the absolute most alluring and profitable remuneration. Simply ensure you don't harm raising support and development endeavors simultaneously.

5. **Training:** Helping colleagues improve themselves and develop in their capacities to procure is just going to support your association. Ensure you have a solid program for preparing, and advancing learning. This can be real estate training or undertaking explicit instruction, just as persuasive and moving occasions.

6. **Offer positive outcomes:** Don't expect that your colleagues feel esteemed on the grounds that you continue paying them, and haven't terminated them yet. They need to realize that their commitment matters, and when they are doing work that is having any kind of effect for the mission. Try not to spare a moment to tell them.

7. **Have the innovation and instruments they need:** Today, incredible ability is attracted to the associations that can enable them to augment their potential. In case you're solid around there, make some clamor about it! Maybe you've grown new, game evolving innovation, or

have put resources into quality devices and frameworks that your rivals haven't. That ought to be a noteworthy advantage. It could notwithstanding get others that are similarly able to dispatch their own dares to turn into a piece of yours.

8. **Solid PR campaign:** like items and administrations, incredible organizations don't sell themselves. They need PR and proactive online notoriety management. Become a magnet for good representatives. What will a Google search or two uncover about you and your group? Is it accurate to say that you are consistently pushing out positive PR? Will top ability in the real estate industry see you and state to themselves "I need to figure out how to be a piece of that organization and mission," and proactively search you out?

   Workers are never again searching for a profession, they're searching for an encounter," and prescribes businesses center around an encounter that is "fulfilling, energizing and enabling.

9. **Referrals:** One of the most ideal approaches to precisely discover top ability in real estate is to use the group and associations you as of now have. This expands the chances they'll be a solid match. Have you connected and inquired as to whether they know anybody that would be a decent resource?

Real estate is an exceptionally aggressive industry, perfect for eager and well informed millennial searching for profession development. The inquiry is, how would we pull in the best ability to your real estate business?

1.) Give adaptability

A focused pay bundle will consistently be appealing. Be that as it may, for twenty to thirty year olds going into real estate and property management, it must be more than the cash. It's not constantly about the dollar for them by any means. Maybe in different enterprises this may prove an alluring draw-car. However, in property management they're not battling for more cash, they're battling for adaptability.

Enabling workers to be adaptable in their calendar implies an association esteems a well-healthy lifestyle and that their welfare is imperative to their manager. Investigate working from home choices and influence innovation to streamline business procedures even outside the workplace.

2.) *Manufacture a solid and comprehensive hierarchical structure*

On enrollment firm Robert Walters' most recent whitepaper: "Pulling in, holding and creating millennial experts", one of the main 3 factors this statistic searches for in an organization is unified with a solid culture. A reasonable and characterized set of hierarchical qualities and culture ought to mirror the millennial's wants of inclusivity, decent variety and open correspondence in the work environment. Not exclusively is having a strong culture rousing for recent college grads, however it likewise attempts to limit strife among them and more seasoned ages.

3.) Make a bona fide brand

Besides informing prospects regarding the organization culture and qualities, it's likewise basic that businesses show it. Advance your organization culture and present it in a great light. New look into from enlistment re-appropriating supplier Manpower Group as of late discovered portion of the Australian occupation searchers accept "a business' image and notoriety are more significant today than it was five years prior".

A helpful and best approach to advance a bona fide brand is through an association's present workers by enjoying and sharing organization internet based life presents on their own systems. This, in any case, should be done naturally in light of the fact that media-sharp Millennials appreciate validness above for all intents and purposes all else.

4.) Go social

Apart from utilizing internet based life channels to advance your image, posting work promotions on social stages as marked pictures or short recordings bears organizations a remarkable chance to draw in and resound with potential representatives.

People matured somewhere in the range of 18 and 39 years, places the most noteworthy in online networking use. Thus, ability securing administrators and expert selection representatives demand the quickest and best approach to enlist Millennials is by concentrating on the social majors – Facebook, Twitter, LinkedIn and Google+.

5.) Advance a reasonable methodology for vocation development

"Twenty to thirty year olds are coming in and expressing that they need a characterized profession. They need to realize where they will be in 10 years' time," as indicated by Adam Hooley. Educating them during the meeting stage that you have a group structure and a lifelong way, and effectively urge new Millennial volunteers to learn and advance are what will engage this statistic.

Tips for procuring and holding a great property management staff

When you're developing your business, perhaps the greatest test is finding the ideal individuals to expedite board. Numerous property supervisors are prepared to take their organization to the following level, however the overwhelming assignment of contracting and holding quality representatives keeps them from making that next stride.

We get it—you're doing combating patterns of high turnover, low joblessness, and furious challenge to enlist top ability. Be that as it may, in case you're set up to settle on the correct choices while contracting, it's less complex than you might suspect to effectively develop your group.

Here are our 4 best contracting tips for property management organizations hoping to pull in and hold the correct individuals to develop your business.

Work a Stand-Out Job Description
Sets of expectations are your organization's first prologue to potential applicants, and it's significant that your activity postings are clear, compact, and precisely mirror the position you're contracting for. A successful set of working

responsibilities causes you to get rid of unfit competitors and draw in top ability.

Ensure your sets of responsibilities check the accompanying boxes:

- **Descriptive and quantifiable.** Your expected set of responsibilities ought to plainly depict work obligations and obligations, just as quantifiable objectives for what achievement will resemble (for example react to occupant demands inside 24 hours).

- **Straightforward necessities.** On the off chance that you've been adopting a reorder strategy to sets of responsibilities, you're likely not contracting effectively. Each new position portrayal ought to indicate the aptitudes and necessities you're searching for—else, you'll be swimming through heaps of unfit candidates with each new position you post.

- **Sell your organization.** Your expected set of responsibilities should respond to this straightforward inquiry for applicants: Why would it be advisable for me to work here? Offer what's extraordinary about working for your organization, for example, your advantages, work environment culture, and accomplishments. It's alright to boast a little and let competitors know why they ought to carry their ability to your business!

Post on the Top Job Boards

Not all occupation sheets are made equivalent. There's such a mind-bending concept as over-posting your employment opportunities, and it brings about an excessive number of candidates and insufficient qualified applicants. Be key about where you post and adhere to the most respectable activity sheets:

- **Free occupation sheets:** To share your activity postings for nothing, attempt destinations like LinkedIn where you'll arrive at a huge number of competitors right away. Look at nearby, online occupation spaces like network Facebook gatherings. In the event that you live close to a junior college or college, there's normally an online activity board to impart postings to understudies and staff.

- **Sponsored employment sheets:** If you're willing to pay a charge, you can support your activity postings on Indeed, Monster, and other major online occupation sheets. Supporting your presents sends your activity on the facade of the line, getting it to more up-and-comers quicker.

Ask the Right Interview Inquiries

You've composed an extraordinary expected set of responsibilities, you've posted it on the correct loads up, and now it's a great opportunity to talk with your up-and-comers. Simple, isn't that so? As a matter of fact, numerous supervisors and owners will disclose to you that it's similarly as overwhelming (if not more so!) to be on the opposite side of the work area during meetings. In the event that you set up the correct inquiries ahead of time, you'll leave with the data you have to settle on the correct choice:

- **Evaluate work abilities.** So as to become familiar with the competitor's activity abilities and encounters, think about posing the accompanying inquiries:

> What has your most prominent accomplishment been grinding away?
> What's an impediment that you've looked at work? How could you beat it?
> How would your associates at your latest occupation depict you? Shouldn't something be said about your administrator?

- **Evaluate employment fit.** Employment fit surveys how a competitor's aptitudes, experience, and desires line up with the position you're attempting to fill. To make sense of if it's a decent coordinate, pose the accompanying inquiries:

  > Why did you leave your latest employment?
  > Why do you need this activity?
  > What are your objectives for what's to come?

- **Evaluate culture fit.** At long last, you'll need to comprehend if the competitor fits in with your group and your vision for the organization's future. Regardless of whether your business has 3 representatives or 30, you need somebody who offers your qualities and your meaning of what achievement resembles. Have a go at inquiring:

  > What are the 3 characteristics that you esteem most in an associate? Shouldn't something be said about in a supervisor?
  > What's the greatest hazard that you've at any point taken, and why?
  > When working in a group domain, which job would you say you are well on the way to take?

Battle High Turnover with Culture and Relationships

When you've contracted the correct up-and-comer, ensure that you have a system set up to hold top ability. There's a ton of turnover in this industry, and the expense of losing a worker is high. Fortunately, there are a few stages you can take to make a flourishing working environment with faithful representatives:

- **Provide preparing openings.** At the point when workers are offered preparing openings, they realize that the organization is put resources into their development. Send your workers to meetings, put resources into structure their ranges of abilities, and make work shadowing openings between representatives.

- **Offer modest pay rates and advantages.** By the day's end, your workers will possibly stay in case you're paying them decently and offering benefits that guarantee their prosperity. Keep in mind, there's an expense to losing somebody—it requires some investment and cash to select, contract, and train each new worker.

Build solid individual connections. Probably the most ideal approaches to connect with representatives and assemble devotion is to become acquainted with them. Make a situation where you get a lot of exposure with every representative to become familiar with their future objectives and what's essential to them. At the point when representatives care about their work connections and realize that you're put resources into their development, they're bound to come to you when there's an issue as opposed to searching for a new position.

CHAPTER IX
HOW TO MANAGE RENTALS OR FIND A PROPERTY MANAGER

While these means are spread out in a particular request, it is conceivable that you may need to manage a portion of the means non-consecutively. Contingent upon what number of properties you oversee or your property points of interest, you may wind up chipping away at Step 7 preceding you arrive at Step 3. That is alright!

No guide, regardless of how extensive, can give you a careful play-by-play of what you should do. Rather, utilize this guide as a general asset to enable you to work through various circumstances as they happen during your time as a property administrator.

Stage 1 - *Buy and Repair*

The initial step of dealing with any investment or rental property is to purchase the property and get it into great fix. On the off chance that your property isn't yet obtained or in rentable condition, these are the two things that you have to take a shot from the outset.

Numerous elements go into purchasing the correct investment property and fixing it to be gainful. Because of what number of variables there are, this guide won't go into those subtleties.

Stage 2 - *Set Prices and Expectations*

When you have control of your rental property and feel that it is prepared to be leased, regardless you have one progressively significant advance to finish before you can begin searching for occupants. It's a great opportunity to set up your rental costs and desires.

1) Statistical surveying In Area

Prior to setting a value, you'll need to look into the normal rental cost in the region and the quantity of rental properties accessible. It's conceivable that you previously did a portion of this exploration during the purchasing procedure.

Make sense of the accompanying:

- What is the normal pay in the territory?
- What is the normal family size?
- What is the normal rental cost?
- Does your area have any extra-unique advantages (i.e., transport line get to, simple parkway access, off-road stopping) that you can charge more for?

As you take in different rentals available and the going rates, you'll have the option to suitably value your rental property.

2) Rundown of Tenant Requirements

Notwithstanding choosing month to month lease, you additionally need to figure out what prerequisites you have for an occupant hoping to move into your property. By having the perfect occupant as of now at the top of the priority list when you start promoting your property, you'll have a superior shot of discovering them.

Think about the accompanying inhabitant qualities, remembering that it is illicit to oppress occupants:

- Minimum pay
- Smoking or no smoking?
- Employment prerequisite
- Credit score least

- Past rental history required?
- Number of references required?

Stage 3 - *Rent Your Property*
Presently it is the most energizing (and troublesome) time of the rental procedure. It's an ideal opportunity to discover new inhabitants to lease your property to!

1) Publicizing
You should publicize your property. Promote wherever that you can; paying for extra introduction will be justified, despite all the trouble. Take a stab at utilizing basic home locales like Zillow just as zone explicit productions, for example, a network magazine.

2) Discovering Good Tenants
Finding any occupant isn't sufficient; you need to discover great inhabitants.
Great occupants regard your property, pay their lease on schedule, and don't cause superfluous issues. It tends to challenge to figure out how to recognize a decent occupant during the meeting procedure, however this ability will be instrumental.

Utilize a rental survey to enable you to see whether every potential occupant is a solid match. Keep in mind that you should adhere to severe principles about what you can and can't get some information about during these meetings. Getting some information about race, handicaps, and family size are essential no-nos. Adhering to reasonable lodging standards is a prerequisite. To locate a decent inhabitant, make certain to do the accompanying:

- Confirm their business area and salary
- Do a credit and historical verification

- Call their references
- Call their previous landowners
- Have one-on-one, in-person discussions with them

Regardless of whether you do these things, you may miss something that shows a terrible inhabitant. Since screening inhabitants can be precarious, you may profit by enlisting an outsider occupant screening administration to enable you to examine all assembled data to locate the best occupants.

3) Composing and Reviewing Rental Contracts

When you have an occupant as a top priority, it will be a great opportunity to sign the rental contract. In the event that you've never set up a rental contract, you will need to assemble some incredible models from online to set up your own.

Then again, procuring a nearby legal advisor to guarantee you don't miss any vital subtleties is an extraordinary thought for your initial couple of agreements. From that point, you can take a shot at your own. Make sure to incorporate data about rental installment timing, ousting strategies, upkeep subtleties, and home principles in the agreement. Moreover, make certain to reveal and gather a security store when concluding the understanding.

4) Survey the Agreement

Before your new inhabitant signs on, you ought to go over the rental concurrence with them. This will give you the two opportunities to pose inquiries and explain data in the agreement to make certain that you each have an unmistakable thought of what the understanding rely on.

5) The Walk-Through

Do a last stroll through either with the occupant or with an outsider target onlooker.

Report whatever number subtleties of the property as could reasonably be expected. These subtleties can be utilized to counteract any contradictions later over harms, and doing the walkthrough with the customer can avert any future issues.

Stage 4 - *Check and Maintain*

When your occupant is moved into the property, your job will turn out to be increasingly inactive, however that doesn't imply that your duties are finished.

As a landowner, you are the occupant's contact point. On the off chance that they need assistance with the property or have an issue, you ought to be accessible to enable them to determine the issue quickly and completely.

1) Rental Visits

There are a couple of advantages to doing rental walkthroughs more than once per year.

To begin with, visiting your inhabitant at their property and checking in with them that everything is functioning admirably is a phenomenal method to keep the lines of correspondence open. There might be little issues springing up that they hadn't yet answered to you; these walkthroughs are the ideal time to increase some more understanding.

Second, doing a walkthrough will enable you to look at the condition of the property. In the event that your inhabitant realizes that you will do bi-yearly walkthroughs, they might be more averse to bring on any harms.

2) Ordinary Maintenance

All properties will require some upkeep. From basic pipes fixes to light apparatus substitution, you can anticipate that your occupant should call you with issues that may spring up all through their residency in your property.

To enable upkeep to happen all the more quickly, set up the accompanying ahead of time:

- List of dependable nearby temporary workers
- Contact data for nearby proprietors who might almost certainly help
- List of fundamental fix issues that you can fix yourself
- Specific support finance
- Schedule ordinary check-ups of machines (AC units, water radiators, etc.)

3) Enormous Repairs

While each proprietor trusts that it won't occur, there is consistently the likelihood that you should take on a major fix while you have your property leased. From a huge pipe burst to a tempest causing broad property harm, enormous fixes may need to occur. In the event that your property needs a critical fix that will drive your occupant to move for a brief period, it is your obligation to give them lodging to whenever that they have officially paid.

You may likewise be required to enable them to pay for elective convenience in forthcoming months relying upon the circumstance. In situations where broad harm has been done to the property, you might need to converse with the occupant about discovering elsewhere to live and finishing your rent understanding early. It is conceivable to approve this sort of progress.

Stage 5 - *Collect Rent*

As a landowner, one of your most noticeable obligations is to gather lease!

Each landowner has an alternate favored strategy for lease accumulation. Some still get checks dropped off or sent to them; others utilize electronic lease gathering administrations that guarantee they get paid on quickly and on schedule.

There are advantages and disadvantages to every strategy, at the end of the day, it's up to you which type you choose. In the event that you do utilize a web based preparing technique for lease gathering, recall that there will be a charge included, and you should work this expense into your rental cost.

1) Raising Rent

Because of increasing expenses in the zone, you may need to raise the lease. Raising the lease while you as of now have occupants in a property may appear to be unimaginable, yet it might be important to do in the event that they are long haul inhabitants who intend to remain for a long time.

Reveal the plausibility of a lease increment to your inhabitants and work with them to check whether they will keep on remaining in the property at the new rate or not.

2) Late Fees

Make certain to uphold a late charge for all late rental installments. On the off chance that your occupant is routinely late with their rental installments, make sure that they know about the probability of ousting should they keep on paying you late.

Occupants will concoct each reason in the book for their late installments, and it's alright to be thoughtful to their motivation at once or another. In any case, when an occupant starts to sequentially pay their lease late, it's an indication that they may never again have the option to bear the cost of your property.

Implementing an unmistakable strategy about late expenses will guarantee that they don't keep on leasing your property on the off chance that they can't bear the cost of it. Your strategy on late charges ought to be clarified in the rental understanding. When giving them notice recently installment expenses, make sure to incorporate the significant area of the rental contract for their reference.

Stage 6 - *Evictions*

No proprietor ever needs to wind up in this position, however it is conceivable that you should experience an expulsion on your properties at some point.
New landowners may have no clue what to do in this circumstance, so it is basic that you do some exploration about neighborhood laws to guarantee that you are observing every one of the guidelines.

It is imperative that you record for ousting and experience the whole court process. Regardless of whether you are disappointed with the time that it takes to get a decision and legitimate ousting continuing, you should pull out to the occupant and record for expulsion in the courts.
Any endeavor to remove the inhabitant yourself (by changing the locks or some other individual activity) can be viewed as a criminal offense.

Spare yourself the issue and rather pursue these essential advances:

- Give them authority see, including to what extent they need to fix the issue that is breaking their rent understanding.
- File the removal with the court if the notice terms are not met.
- Do not acknowledge installment in the event that you are petitioning for ousting, as it can invalidate the expulsion procedure.
- Read nearby laws to make certain you don't disrupt any norms.
- Hire an attorney if the laws are mistaking for you.
- Wait for the court administering and nearby sheriff to play out the genuine expulsion.

Stage 7 - *Accounting*

Another angle to property management that you may not be comfortable with is the measure of charges and other bookkeeping data that you will deal with.

In the event that you had a property management organization, they would deliver this data in reports for you, yet doing it individually can be increasingly confounded.

To make your business bookkeeping simpler, pursue these tips and deceives:

1. Hire a bookkeeper to do your assessments; the expense is justified, despite all the trouble. They'll enable you to expand findings and guarantee a spotless record.
2. Keep an exhaustive record off all cash spent on support and other fundamental property upkeep; these are deductible.
3. Set up explicit ledgers for your costs of doing business to guarantee that your own funds don't get stirred up in the business accounts.
4. Set aside cash to cover charges and different expenses that may astonish you.

It's Time to be The Best Property Manager

You've chosen to figure out how to oversee rental properties for yourself, and that is a remarkable accomplishment! Since you know the fundamentals of property management, the best way to end up experienced at each progression is to place this learning energetically.

Keep in mind that in its most moderate structure, property management requires just a couple of basic advances:

- Buy and fix a property
- Set up a rental expense and occupant prerequisites
- Find occupants and lease the house to them
- Maintain the property
- Collect lease and cover government expenses
- Profit

Try not to progress toward becoming overpowered at the idea of dealing with your properties. Being a proprietor is remunerating work, and you can help improve your own riches by remaining sorted out and alert all through the procedure. You can be an extraordinary proprietor; you should simply attempt!

Top Secrets to Finding the Best Property Manager

Possibly you want to deal with the property yourself? Maybe.
In any case, on the off chance that you utilize my tips to locate a remarkable management organization, they'll set aside you more cash than the charge you're paying them.
Consider that. You'll do less work, however set aside more cash.

The ideal rental property management organization acquires their management charge and that's only the tip of the iceberg. They show improvement over you could in the event that you did it without anyone else's help.

They have more involvement:

- Finding inhabitants
- Dealing with killjoy occupants
- Collecting late lease

- Doing removals
- Finding reasonable costs and getting limits from contractual workers
- Knowing what fixes are essential (and superfluous) for rentals
- Knowing which areas are best for rentals
- Pricing rentals
- And a whole lot more…

To emphasize, these organizations wind up being worth definitely more than their charges simply through their contacts, mastery, and comprehension of the rental market.

Once more, this is possibly valid on the off chance that you locate the correct management organization. There are likewise a lot of terrible ones that will cost more cash and be as much fill in as doing it without anyone else's help.

That is the place following these tips come in! There are a lot of books and blog entries about overseeing rental properties yourself.

What a cerebral pain! You are paying a property management organization for specialization and mastery that you can't copy by perusing books and online journals yourself. This will sound sales rep y, however it's valid. It is working incredible for me, and it can work for you, or anybody you realize that requirements it. I claim twenty single-family homes and they are generally being overseen by a similar rental property management organization. I've built up a framework and fabricated a group in the course of recent years that is really working for me (truly and metaphorically).

The most significant piece of this framework is the rental property management group.
Here are privileged insights for finding the ideal one.

1. *Peruse the fine print*

When you procure a rental property management organization, they make you sign an agreement. You need to peruse this agreement cautiously. There is something explicit I need you to look for.

Ensure they don't make it difficult to fire them. I don't get my meaning by this?
The agreement will have something in it that decides under what conditions you can end the rental property management contract with them.
In the event that you end the agreement, you may need to pay a couple of more month of their management expenses. It might even say you need to pay the remainder of the year. Comprehend this language. On the off chance that you feel they are performing seriously, and need to quit utilizing them, ensure you see the amount it will cost to leave. You have to likewise comprehend what move you have to make to legitimately drop the agreement. You may need to accomplish something recorded as a hard copy or by enlisted mail.

I arranged having this part of the agreement removed from my agreement. In the event that I was discontent with the management organization's administration, I had the option to end without paying any extra-long stretches of management charges.
Ensure you have the alternative to dispose of the property management organization if important, and ensure it doesn't cost you to an extreme.

2. Check their expenses

Start off by taking a gander at their management contract, and understanding their expense structure.
The most essential charge to comprehend is how they would charge management. Most normally it is a level of lease. 10% of lease is very normal, however I've seen numerous spots charge less. 8% isn't unprecedented.

It's much the same as some other expense structure throughout everyday life, be that as it may. At the point when an organization charges 8% rather than 10%, you may see that in some other piece of the expense structure, they might be more costly than a contender. They discover elsewhere to compensate for it.

A genuine case of this is shown with my present rental property management organization. They charge 10%, which some may state is high, yet they don't charge an expense for discovering inhabitants and marking a rent. They additionally don't charge an expense for leaving a rent once it lapses. A great deal of other property management organizations do.

Numerous organizations charge a month's lease, or possibly a large portion of a month's lease for marking a rent. This can be significant in ascertaining your costs.

My turnover rates in Montgomery, Alabama are very high. The normal turnover is between 1 ½ to 2 years. It would cost me a fortune to pay a month's lease each time that occurs, so having this incorporated into my 10% expense is brilliant.

In the event that you were in a territory where turnover was lower, possibly an expense of one month's lease wouldn't work out as being not good enough for you. A few people lease a similar house for five or ten years. See how your management organization will charge you for utilizing outside temporary workers. They may charge you the expense of the contractual worker in addition to a rate markup. They may likewise have their very own contractual workers that they have their own charge framework with. Ensure you get it and contrast it with other management organizations in the region.

The procedure of ousting is diverse state-to-state so to what extent it takes and the amount it expenses can fluctuate enormously. The expense of court and charges that should be paid additionally differ similarly. Solicit them to clarify the procedure from removal obviously to you. You have to see to what extent it takes regularly and most dire outcome imaginable. You additionally need to see the amount it will cost you in the two cases to get somebody out of the house. Ask how regularly it occurs and what their screening procedure is to attempt to keep away from it.

3. *Would you be able to confide in them?*

The primary spot to look is checking with online sources.
Check the better business authority. You'll have the option to check whether they are enrolled and if there are any protests against them and how these grumblings were settled.

Next, do loads of research online. Check for surveys on them or potentially grievances about them. Be careful with an organization that appears to have no online nearness of any sort. That is a notice sign. They are excessively new, or concealing something. You have to check the better business authority, google their organization name, and utilize each other online asset you can consider to perceive what individuals are stating about them.

Next, request references. Disclose to them you might want authorization to converse with different investors who utilize their management administrations. In a perfect world you can converse with at any rate three. Address a portion of their leaseholders too. Perceive how they are treated by the management organization. These are reference that the property management organization is giving you, and these just have constrained handiness. There is an inclination. They realize you are calling and why, and they feel obliged to express pleasant words. They may even be "companions" of the management organization or investors or leaseholders that show signs of improvement than different clients.

For what reason does that make a difference?
Since you need an example of what the normal investor or tenant is being dealt with like.
In a perfect world, you will figure out how to build up your very own references. You do this by asking the reference that you were given on the off chance that they know any other person you can converse with. This might be somebody who will give an increasingly legitimate or unprejudiced supposition.

The references you create yourself are more powerful than the ones given to you from the organization.
In the event that the organization is hesitant to give references, this is known as a piece of information. You might need to reexamine. Likewise, if the management organization doesn't work with any investors, this may likewise be of concern. You'll be the first. That doesn't mean it's a no-go, yet it implies they don't have much

understanding and you won't have the advantage of addressing different investors who can vouch for previously being satisfied with their administration.

How amenable would they say they are? How expert would they say they are with my request? These are what I'm deciding from these telephone calls.

A major issue would be never finding solutions by email and not breaking through to an individual by telephone. Another would be inconsiderate or amateurish responses to questions. I would likewise be concerned in the event that they appeared to be fine with leasing to individuals with really awful credit or no pay. When I've fulfilled that test, I proceed onward to conversing with the owners of the property management organization.

4. Meet the owners and workers

You need to do this face to face. Specifically evaluating their dependability is something you can't put a cost on. In the event that you are doing this from a far distance, at that point skype or video is your final hotel, yet I would contend you would fly or drive out and get this going face to face. Try not to do it by telephone, you need to have the option to look at one another without flinching and become more acquainted with them on an individual level.

It's a great opportunity to play twenty inquiries. I'm not constraining you to twenty, which is only the name of that game you at times play in the vehicle on long travels. Set up an extensive rundown of inquiries that you need to pose about how they will deal with each possible circumstance you can consider. All that you are stressed over as a landowner, you will approach in what capacity they will handle it for you. Pets, awful credit, late charges, somebody who junks the house, somebody who won't move out, claims, atomic war, what occurs if this organization fails, anything you can consider.

Here's a rundown of inquiries concocted to begin you off.

- How old is your organization?
- How did you begin in overseeing real estate?
- How much experience do every one of you have in the real estate business? Property management business? Give me subtleties.
- How numerous rental properties do you claim yourselves?
- How numerous rental properties do you oversee for investors?
- How a wide range of real estate investors would you say you are overseeing for?
- Will you let me address a portion of these investors about their experience working with you?
- How do removals work in this state and city? To what extent does it take regularly and most pessimistic scenario? How would you handle expulsions and by what method will I be charged for it regularly and most pessimistic scenario?
- What are your opportunity rates?
- Do you have your very own contractual workers that work for you solely? What number of and how would you charge me to utilize them?
- What is your criteria and pay prerequisites for screening inhabitants?
- What is your pet arrangement?
- Can I see an example rental report that you send investors every month?

- Will you let me address a portion of your inhabitants about their experience working with you?
- Do you have an arrangement for my properties on the off chance that you choose to quit overseeing rentals?

You need and anticipate that genuine answers should every one of these inquiries. On the off chance that there is hesitance or hesitance to reply, not a decent sign. As I would like to think, you don't need a management organization that is pristine and doesn't have any understanding. You likewise don't need a management organization that is so enormous, they are not willing to meet with you and answer these inquiries. In the event that you are simply one more number to them, you'll presumably get poor administration. They ought to be eager to meet with you and answer addresses like this to get your business as an investor.

Now, ideally you have enough data about the property management organization to realize you could contract them. It do as well. There is another significant advance that is just conceivable once they are enlisted and effectively overseeing it for you. It is guaranteeing them superb administration.

5. Guarantee you are getting quality administration

You have done all your schoolwork and contracted what you accept to be a quality organization. The work doesn't end there. You are going to discover they do things that you don't care for. This might be their strategic approaches, awful choices, bookkeeping issues, slow in taking care of opportunities, or any number of issues

Interestingly, you plainly convey what you are discontent with, and get them to fix that conduct. Keep in mind, you are paying them a charge to get an administration, and you anticipate certain things for that expense. These sort obviously redresses ought not out of the ordinary. Basically, you are preparing them to be the ideal property chiefs.

In working with our management organization, we once in a while find that things are uncertain from the budget report every month how cash was spent. We quickly talk with the owners and explain why there is disarray over where cash went a month ago. This consistently brings about an increasingly improved monetary report the next month. This makes recording charges and understanding our benefits and misfortunes a lot simpler.

Another genuine model is the treatment of opening. In the event that you see that it is taking the management organization longer than it ought to fill an opportunity, call them and get some information about it. Check and perceive how they have it publicized. Get some information about the cost and in the event that you should possibly offer a move in exceptional or some sort of motivating force to get it leased.

This should bring about improved dealing with in opening as time goes on. In the event that it doesn't, at that point you must have increasingly genuine discussions with them. Opening can be an intense issue for you, particularly in the event that you have a home loan to pay.

Do you recollect my model from early where I terminated a management organization since they cited me a few thousand dollars to fix the stairs, and when I send a jack of all trades over, he fixed it for $50? I would prescribe now and again planning something comparable only for keep everyone genuine.

On the off chance that there is some kind of enormous offered going on, you ought to get a couple of statements from the management organization. You would then straightforwardly tell the management organization that you are likewise sending over a temporary worker that a companion prescribed to get an offer too. You need just do this every once in a while as a method for ensuring their offers are reasonable. It's classified "trust, yet check". Trust however check basically implies I don't confide in you yet, so I need to confirm. There is nothing amiss with that. Individuals that look and appear to be straightforward do obscure stuff and now and then frustrate us. Remember to trust, however confirm. I think on the off chance that you get singed by your management organization along these lines, it's a terrible sign. A cheat is a cheat. You need to fire them.

A few people will choose to oversee properties themselves. As I referenced before, an exceptional property management organization has so much experience and contacts, that they more than compensate for the charges you pay them. You profit over the long haul by utilizing that learning and experience.

By following my tips, you will get rid of the rotten ones, and discover extraordinary management organizations that will progress toward becoming accomplices in your real estate business. You will profit for them, and they will produce noteworthy automated revenue for you.

It will be a genuine and success win in the organization.

CHAPTER X
THE BEST EXIT STRATEGIES TO CONSIDER

Numerous individuals enter the real estate contributing business for the budgetary advantages this market offers – it's an obvious fact that the general purpose of buying investment properties is to profit through gratefulness or lease in the years to come. No effective real estate investor enters the market without building up a productive plan of action (plan) – subsequently, having a leave procedure before obtaining a real estate investment property.

What Is a Real Estate Exit system?

As the name recommends, a real estate leave technique is an arrangement where the real estate investor expects to evacuate him/herself from a real estate contributing arrangement. Basically, a leave methodology is a thought as what the real estate investor will do with the investment property.

Some leave systems are arranged by real estate investors as a feature of the first investment choice (plan of action/plan). Then again, some property investors start considering a leave methodology once they have a clearer image of the investment and things start to unwind. Nonetheless, the best guidance for real estate investors is to design a leave system before buying investment properties.

In many cases, property investors neglect to realize the significance of setting up a leave technique when making a real estate contributing arrangement. All in all, what makes leave procedures so significant?

The Importance of a Real Estate Exit Strategy

There are various causes that drive real estate investors into executing exit system plans:

1. Determining a suitable real estate leave methodology not exclusively will give real estate investors a strategy, yet it will likewise limit pending dangers. At the point when property investors assess potential leave procedures before acquiring investment properties, they realize the dangers related with the investment and ability to evade them.

2. Having a particular leave procedure is pivotal to progress, as the right approach will result in augmented benefits. It's never savvy to enter a real estate contributing arrangement without having an unmistakable comprehension of how you will benefit from the real estate property when leaving from the contributing arrangement. Along these lines, having a money related objective and a leave procedure can spare you thousands – if not millions – of dollars all through your real estate contributing profession.

3. What on the off chance that you obtained an investment property and some time later you realized that real estate contributing isn't really your thing? Or on the other hand in case you're not ready to stay aware of the requests of the real estate contributing business sector? Or on the other hand in the event that you've lost your enthusiasm and now your real estate property is turning into a weight or is simply not worth your endeavors? These are reasons why having a leave technique before buying investment properties is significant.

4. Unexpected crises can influence anybody, including real estate investors. An investor may discover him/herself stayed by a catastrophe and in urgent need of money. In this circumstance, a real estate leave system will help sell the property quicker and money out.

5. Real estate leave systems are likewise advantageous for property investors who are thinking about to grow their real estate investment portfolio and have greater investments. This is presumably one of the most widely recognized motivations to actualize a leave technique as it'll give property investors a comprehension of how to deal with these distinctive investment properties and the proper behavior on the off chance that one of them isn't giving return regarding rental pay or appreciation.

Basically, neglecting to set up a real estate leave system can prompt diminishing potential benefits and expanding dangers simultaneously. Understanding way out methodologies before obtaining investment properties will guarantee property investors that they will love entering the real estate contributing business sector. The inquiry that is left to answer is: What are the most widely recognized leave methodologies that real estate investors pursue?

Top Real Estate Exit Strategies

Understanding and picking the correct exit technique will eventually influence how effective you will be in your real estate contributing vocation.

Exit Strategy #1: *Fix-and-Flip*

This real estate leave methodology normally brings about the most elevated net revenues, as it enables the real estate investor to sell the real estate property at full market esteem. It includes obtaining investment properties that need fix (beneath market esteem), redesigning them, and afterward selling them for more than the first investment costs (price tag in addition to fix costs).

Remember that real estate investors who try to execute this exit methodology ought to know about market patterns, and able to do rapidly increasing the value of real estate investment properties.

Exit Strategy #2: *Buy-and-Hold*

This leave technique is well known for real estate investors hoping to develop value in a real estate property. It's like that of fix-and-flip; in any case, rather than selling the revamped property, the real estate investor holds it for a while and lease it out to get month to month income (rental pay). As gratefulness and value develop, these investment properties can be sold for a benefit.

Exit Strategy #3: *Wholesaling*

Essentially, a discount arrangement is the point at which a real estate investor (distributer) goes about as the mediator between a property vender and a property purchaser. Fundamentally, a real estate distributer finds and rapidly sells a modest real estate property for an overall revenue. Real estate wholesalers place the investment property under a buy contract and after that sell this agreement (or "allocate" it) to the purchaser for a little benefit.

This exit methodology is exceptionally looked for after by property investors when they have to end a real estate contributing arrangement since it spares investors' time.

Exit Strategy #4: *Seller Financing*

This is an amazing technique for leaving a real estate property while proceeding to deliver a benefit. For this situation, the vender funds the real estate contributing arrangement and goes about as a bank. The vender and the purchaser trade a promissory note including a financing cost and a reimbursement plan. This exit procedure benefits venders as they are granted regularly scheduled installments to cover the home loan credit and their arrival on investment increments through premium pay.

Exit Strategy #5: *Rent to Own (Lease Option)*

This kind of leave procedures permits the real estate property owner to lease the investment property to an occupant, however with the alternative to buy it after a set timeframe. Now and again, a part of the regularly scheduled installments is put towards the price tag of the home.

Effective Methods to Choose the Best Exit Strategy

The choice of which one of the previously mentioned real estate contributing way out techniques to utilize isn't as straightforward as it might show up. There is no standard to separate between them. Moreover, there are a few components to mull over when arranging a leave methodology, basically the real estate investors' commonality with their:

- Short and long haul objectives
- Experience level

- Time to close
- Purchase cost
- Property esteem
- Condition of the property
- Market conditions
- Supply and request
- Financing choices
- Profit potential

Understanding these elements will enable a real estate investor to figure out which of the real estate exit methodologies he/she ought to use.

Variables That Could Ruin an Exit Strategy

It is significant for real estate investors to comprehend that specific components may demolish an arranged real estate leave methodology, for example,

- Depreciation
- Tenant issues bringing about lost lease
- Unexpected support expenses can counterbalance benefits
- Poor property management that diminishes the worth and potential income
- A particular absence of interest, or bombed escrow, or the retreating from a loan specialist may that keeps the investment property from being flipped

By and by, effective real estate investors can check these potential deterrents by having different exit strategies. Things can change at some random minute; along these lines, having a reinforcement plan is a smart thought.

Before making a real estate contributing arrangement and acquiring investment properties, real estate investors ought to see how to exit the investment property and when to offer it to make a benefit – as this is the general purpose of real estate. An exit methodology is a system to enable the real estate investor to cash-out of the investment property with least trouble.